Stéphane Mallarmé

Titles in the series Critical Lives present the work of leading cultural figures of the modern period. Each book explores the life of the artist, writer, philosopher or architect in question and relates it to their major works.

In the same series

Stéphane Mallarmé

Roger Pearson

REAKTION BOOKS

In affectionate memory of Malcolm Bowie

Published by Reaktion Books Ltd
33 Great Sutton Street
London EC1V ODX, UK

www.reaktionbooks.co.uk

First published 2010

Printed and bound in Great Britain
by CPI Antony Rowe, Chippenham, Wiltshire

British Library Cataloguing in Publication Data
Pearson, Roger
    Stephane Mallarme. – (Critical lives)
    1. Mallarme, Stephane, 1842–1898.
    2. Poets, French 19th century Biography.
    I. Title II. Series
    841.8-DC22

ISBN 978 1 86189 659 9

Contents

Paul Nadar, *Stéphane Mallarmé, c.* 1890.

Note on References and Translations

References to Mallarmé's work have been included in the text using the following abbreviated forms:

Corr.   *Correspondance*, ed. Henri Mondor and Jean-Pierre Richard
        (vol. I), Henri Mondor and Lloyd James Austin (vols II–XI)
        (11 vols, Paris: Gallimard, 1959–85)

DSM   *Documents Stéphane Mallarmé*, ed. Carl Paul Barbier et al.
        (7 vols, Paris: Nizet, 1968–80)

OC   *Œuvres complètes*, ed. Bertrand Marchal (2 vols, Paris:
        Gallimard, Bibliothèque de la Pléiade, 1998–2003)

All translations are my own.

Introduction: Critical Moments

'Crisis means health as well as sickness.' (*oc*, II. 663)

During the second half of the nineteenth century the French poet
Stéphane Mallarmé lived a life that was highly and repeatedly
critical. He underwent his own crisis of body and mind in 1866
at the age of twenty-four, and it marked him profoundly. In 1885
he reached a 'critical moment in my life (when I must shine forth
once and for all)' and resolved to complete the 'Drama, as I see it
in my dream, for the best way to describe something is to show
it in its finished form' (*Corr.*, II. 294). In May 1889 he talked of the
'full-blown crisis' that verse itself was undergoing (*Corr.*, III. 312),
and later he gave the title of 'Crise de vers' (Verse Crisis) to a
complex and considered statement of his own poetics in which
he related the controversial innovations of *vers libre* (free verse) to
the political and religious crises of his age. Moreover this particular text exemplified a new genre, the *poëme critique*, which he
himself had created in order to address such critical moments:
a dense form of unversified but poetically charged writing, at
once lapidary and lacunary, in which language enacts within the
proper bounds of syntax – by homophony, etymological play, and
unconventional punctuation – the dialectical tensions informing
the questions under consideration. Whether in verse or prose,
Mallarmé maintained, poetry is 'a language of crisis' (*Corr.*, VI.
185, n. 1).

By his influence on contemporaries through his practice and personal example, and later on posterity through his bequeathed *œuvre*, Mallarmé became also a critical point of reference: for poets, for literary theorists, for historians of 'modernity', for readers and creative artists of every kind. And, with a decade of the twenty-first century already gone, a key point of reference he remains.

But whereas, as its etymology suggests, a crisis marks a decisive juncture in the flow of time – as it might be, in the progress of a fever or in the life of the body politic – the great originality of Mallarmé's writing lies in the fact that the decisions are never taken. 'To be or not to be . . .'. In his view *Hamlet* is the greatest of plays because it figures a human being 'inbetween': poised between action and inaction, madness and sanity, childhood and maturity. Thereby Shakespeare's tragedy represents the fundamental indeterminacy of our earthly existence (there is no other) and forbears to foist easy solutions on its audience. 'Suspens' and 'attente' – suspense and expectancy – were Mallarmé's own words for this artful simulation of our critical ontological uncertainty.

'Mystery' was another. From the Greek verb meaning 'to close', the word designates that about which initiates must keep their mouths firmly shut, and Mallarmé performed his poetic mysteries as a sequence of compelling glimpses and delicate deferrals. For him the poet's role amidst a welter of meaningless contingency is to create linguistic patterns that may just convince us, for a nanosecond, that they do mean something, that we have seen beyond the veil of the here and now. Like that opening scene in *Macbeth*, as he noted towards the end of his life, where by seeming accident, as though the curtain had risen prematurely, we snatch brief sight of the fateful witches, the cackling scriptwriters of our human destiny. 'Only connect . . .'. Like stars in a constellation the poet's linguistic patterns are no more than an anthropomorphic projection of the human longing to find shape and make sense.

Yet they do matter. The poet orchestrates that longing and provides a therapy of reading that matters also.

Since the dawn of time the primordial critical moment has been sunset. Like many of his contemporaries Mallarmé was attracted to the idea that all religions and all myths are narratives of the solar passage, what he calls the 'solar drama'. Fearful of the dark and of death, the primitive mind came to see in the setting and rising of the sun a symbolic enactment of the principle of cyclicity, a rhythm of eternal being in which the stark fact of mortality ceased to have the final word and became implicated in a syntax that culminated in a new dawn and an endless future. Witness also the diurnal death of our only-begotten sun, how it brings a darkness that permits innumerable other suns to shine.

In his writing Mallarmé repeatedly figures what he calls these 'pure rhythmic motifs of being' (*oc*, II. 29), not only describing them but also performing them in his formal and verbal procedures. His first move is always to switch off the light of the obvious ('écarte la lampe', he tells us, move that lamp away), plunging his readers into 'obscurity'. But then he inveigles us, by suggestion and proffered vista, towards some tentative and 'suspenseful' intimations of presence and brilliance, a constellation of potential meanings and connections that far exceed our trivial daylight understandings. To read Mallarmé – and there is no fallacy in saying that he intended this – is to behold the void and then to see something within and perhaps beyond it. At first he called this something 'Beauty', later the 'Idea': 'rhythm between relationships' (*Corr.*, VI. 26).

For Mallarmé, language is our most powerful instrument for shaping the contingent data of human experience into patterns that offer tantalizing prospects of a meaningfulness that transcends the random banality of the given. Ever alert to etymology, he treasured the derivation of 'poetry' from the Greek verb meaning to make, fashion, or fabricate: hence also his recurrent use of the word 'fiction' (from the Latin) to describe his own writings.

'Literature' is a 'fashioning' of letters (and the sounds they represent) into 'poems' and 'fictions', figments that derive their authenticity from maximizing the potential of language, mobilizing as consciously as possible its phonetic, morphological, syntactic and lexical 'virtualities' and orchestrating them, like a composer, in therapeutic patterns of descent and ascent, despair and joy, bafflement and insight. Such an activity may lack all kind of transcendental sanction, and poems may indeed be fictions and fabrications. But if literature is a lie, it is 'the Glorious Lie' (*Corr.*, I. 208).

How, then, should a poet live a poet's life, a 'critical' life? What indeed *are* poets? What do they do? What *should* they do? Can we all be poets? These ticklish questions are often addressed by Mallarmé: seriously, never earnestly, sometimes playfully. Writing in 1895, at the age of 52, he tells with wry, avuncular charm of young people coming to him for advice. Would-be poets presumably, for why else would they come to him, these 'camarades' – etymologically, these 'room-mates' (in 'stanzas' of verse and as guests in his own living-room during his famous Tuesday gatherings)? They feel a need to *do* something, they want to make a difference. But what have they got in mind exactly? What has roused them from their 'sedentary musing'? They don't seem like the active – let alone activist – sort, even if they do happen to enjoy the current vogue for bicycling and may even throw the odd bomb. Perhaps they just want to prove that they exist – 'something of which not one of us is initially quite certain' – and to do so by 'causing among many [people] a stir that gives you in return the thrill that you were its originating principle'. There are two ways of doing this: either you spend a lifetime in private and anonymous thinking so that ultimately your work 'bursts in multiple form' upon the world; or else you can, by using the ephemeral means of 'journals and their whirlwind', 'determine a force in one direction [*sens*: also 'sense', 'meaning'], *any* direction/sense/meaning, which when variously

countered leaves [you with] the immunity of having no effect.'
The choice is yours, he concludes: 'plenitude' or 'haste'.

A poet *writes*: mere 'meditation' is evanescent and literally
leaves no trace. But the act of writing is to be envisaged not as the
placing of a luminous 'stellar alphabet' upon a 'field of obscurity'
but rather as the 'presentation' of a 'fold of dark lace' that 'retains
the infinite' and 'assembles distant traceries wherein lies a luxury
to be inventoried' . . . 'with the something or nothing of mystery,
indispensable, that abides, expressed, just a little.' Being a poet is
not easy, therefore! Removed from the realm of 'exceptional' deeds
and 'vulgar proceedings', the poet must live a form of 'omission',
indeed almost a 'death'. For his 'exploits' are performed in the
world of dream . . . 'so as not to bother anyone'.

This self-deprecating advice comes from a 'critical poem'
entitled *L'Action restreinte* (*oc,* II. 21–8), meaning at once action
that is restricted or limited, and also restrained. This 'poem' had
originally been published – under the simple title *L'Action* – in a
journal, thereby creating uncertainty as to which of the two choices
our poet had himself adopted. Indeed Mallarmé eventually
described his 'critical poems' as being essentially newspaper articles
with the boring, wordy bits left out. And this is typical. He addresses
serious questions, and he has some far-reaching answers to them:
original, complex, and influential answers. But never solemn or
portentous ones. Still less was he pretentious. For he had a playful
and ironic cast of mind that protected him – except perhaps for
that one 'crisis' period in his mid-to-late twenties – from taking life
and poetry *too* seriously. And even then friends had tried to tease
him out of it: 'Are you still juggling with those pet snakes of yours,
the Absolute, and Being, and Nothingness?', asked Eugène Lefébure
in a letter of early August 1866. For Mallarmé poetry was the
'supreme Game' (*oc,* I. 2), the 'literary game *par excellence*' (*oc,*
I. 788), but a game withal; and each thought or utterance, like
each act of living, was a throw of the dice in the maelstrom of time.

Mallarmé's own life was lived as a series of critical moments, and it falls to his biographer to recount not only the vicissitudes of his poetic ambitions and achievements but also the circumstances from which they sprang. Famously he told his friend Henri Cazalis in May 1867: 'I am perfectly dead' (*Corr.*, i. 20), meaning that as a poet he had decided to abandon the Romantic conception of the lyric as a mode of self-expression and had resolved instead to 'cede the initiative to words' ('Crise de vers', *oc*, ii. 211): that is, to see what words had to say and to let them say it, as richly and 'connectedly' as possible. Accordingly Mallarmé became the very epitome of the 'Death of the Author', and for many he is still the ivory-tower poet of Symbolist legend, 'sculpting his own tomb' (*oc*, ii. 700) in blind disregard of the gas bill and the latest football results. And yet even as he was informing Cazalis of his 'death', he was also nervously proclaiming the hope that he would survive long enough to complete his 'Great Work'. Mallarmé lived his poetic ambitions daily and as a man profoundly engaged in what it meant to live the life of a human being. For life is all we have: 'the magnificent act of living', he once called it (*oc*, ii. 188). As his daughter Geneviève fondly recalled in 1916: 'he was a stranger to nothing that lent charm to living. With his family and close friends he was always on the most immediate and heart-to-heart terms.' In fact, already aware of the legend that had grown up during his lifetime, she had told him with great delight in April 1897: 'You're no solitary monk. Absolutely not' (*dsm*, ii. 166). And so we shall find.

1

Classrooms

In one of several ribald poems written during his late teens Mallarmé speculates on how great poets are made. His carefully constructed Petrarchan sonnet ('Parce que de la viande . . .') might read thus in plain translated prose:

> Because the meat had been roasted just so, because the newspaper carried the story of a rape, because the maid had forgotten to button her collar over an ignoble and ill-furnished bust, because from a bed as big as a vestry he can see an antique couple disporting on a mantlepiece clock, or simply because he cannot sleep and his leg happens immodestly to brush against another between the sheets, a simpleton places his cold and unmoist wife beneath him, rubs his roundhead on this night-capped doll, and gets puffing and panting to work; and because one night, without passion or raging storm, these two human beings coupled as they went to sleep, O Shakespeare! O Dante!, a poet may be born!

But the making of the man who would one day write the more subtly erotic *L'Après-midi d'un faune* (The Afternoon of a Faun) seems to have been an altogether more concerted event. Stéphane Mallarmé was born at approximately 7 a.m. on Friday, 18 March 1842. His parents, Numa (1805–1863) and Félicie (1819–1847) had married exactly nine months earlier and lived with Félicie's parents,

Camille Delagrange, *Stéphane Mallarmé as a Child*, pastel.

André and Fanny Desmolins (1789–1865, 1799–1869), at 12 rue Laferrière in central Paris, where the baby was delivered.

Numa Mallarmé, the fifth of eight children, was a successful civil servant and came from a long line of public administrators. He worked in that department of the Ministry of Finance which, since the 1789 Revolution, had been responsible for the registration and taxation of property and commercial transactions. His own

Camille Delagrange, *Maria Mallarmé as a Child*, pastel.

father, François Mallarmé (1776–1851), had been a provincial tax official in this so-called Administration de l'Enregistrement et des Domaines and was now living in retirement in Dijon, while his great-uncle had been President of the National Convention when it voted the execution of Louis XVI on 20 January 1793. Likewise Numa's new father-in-law occupied a high-ranking position in this same department of the Enregistrement, for which he had been appointed to the Legion of Honour. In fact, after a series of promotions that had recently culminated in a career-defining move from Chartres to Paris, Numa the aspiring civil servant had married the boss's daughter – just as his father-in-law himself had done in January 1818. One day baby Stéphane would no doubt follow in this proud family tradition of bureaucratic service to the nation and find a nice tax-inspector's daughter with whom to share a seemly marital bed.

Two years later, at the same address, Félicie Mallarmé gave birth to her second child, Maria, on 25 March. With the assistance of the Desmolins the couple bought a large, two-storey, chalet-style house at 44 rue de Ranelagh, in the increasingly fashionable quarter of Passy. One of twenty detached residences currently under construction in a gated development called the Hameau de Boulainvilliers, their new home was to have a large garden and be surrounded by trees and shrubbery. It would be like moving to the country, and they duly did so towards the end of the following year. One of their neighbours, at 38 rue de Ranelagh, would soon afterwards be Numa's half-sister Herminie du Saussey, his step-mother's daughter by an earlier marriage to a Norman baron and now a kindly spinster in her early fifties. Her faintly aristocratic lineage was in keeping with the aspirations of the new neighbour-hood, which also counted wealthy English and American visitors among its residents. The Mallarmés had moved out and up, and the future seemed bright.

But in 1847, on 2 August, Félicie Mallarmé died. She was only 28, her son Stéphane but five years old. The evidence is limited, but it seems that she had been ill for some time: perhaps tuberculosis (she coughed a lot), but more probably rheumatoid arthritis. She and her husband had only just returned from a visit to Rome, Félicie clutching a crucifix blessed by the Pope himself. Had this journey been the last wish of a dying woman in search of a miracle?

The Desmolins moved to Passy soon afterwards to provide what support they could, and were glad of the change of address when revolution broke out on the streets of central Paris in February 1848. King Louis-Philippe, fearing the fate of Louis xvi, abdicated. Assuming the unimaginative but helpfully unremarkable alias of 'Mr Smith', he fled to England, where he died (in Surrey) some two years later. The Second Republic was proclaimed on 25 February but the unrest continued, and Numa Mallarmé found himself obliged to enlist in the ranks of a Home Guard whose duty was to protect the inhabitants of Passy from insurgent radicals. Peace returned with the election of Prince Louis-Napoléon Bonaparte as President in December.

Meanwhile a more intimate and far-reaching revolution had occurred in the Mallarmé household. Numa's father had found his 42-year-old son a new bride in Dijon: Anna Mathieu, the nineteen-year-old daughter of a retired artillery officer of his acquaintance. Numa took his two young children to meet her, and on 27 October 1848 the couple wed. Their marriage settlement recorded that while Numa owned the house at Ranelagh and some 10,500 francs in other assets (about £30,000 in today's terms), his holdings included his first wife's dowry of 20,500 francs, which would be owing to Stéphane and Maria when they reached the age of majority.

The Desmolins were upset by the rapidity with which their deceased daughter had been replaced, but their former son-in-law, a rather stern and unbending sort, had made an excellent choice. For Anna was the very opposite of the wicked stepmother, being a kind and understanding young woman who felt keenly the emotional needs and vulnerabilities of her new stepchildren, aged six and three. Stéphane and Maria had been staying with their grandparents since their mother's death, but now they moved back to the family home. After a while, perhaps at their grandmother's concerned or possessive instigation, Maria went back to live with her while Stéphane remained with his father and stepmother. Fanny Desmolins, the devout wife of a lapsed husband, had strict views on how children should be brought up and did not trust Anna to be sufficiently firm. She ensured also that Stéphane visit her regularly in his free time, to be doted on with discipline.

Mallarmé's first extant poem dates from about this period. The neighbourhood of Passy was inhabited by several leading writers and artists, including Charles Dubois Davesnes, a successful playwright and theatre director. His second daughter, Fanny, who would soon become a noted sculptress and was then in her early twenties, had befriended Stéphane, helping him with his reading and even teaching him the rudiments of French versification. Hence the poem which he wrote as a 'thank you':

> *Ma chère Fanny*
> *Ma bonne amie*
> *Je te promets d'être sage*
> *À tout âge*
> *Et de toujours t'aimer.*
> *Stéphane Mallarmé.*

The syllable count is irregular and the rhymes imperfect, but the thought is there: 'My dear Fanny, my good friend, I promise to be good, as long as I live, and to love you always. Stéphane Mallarmé.' Here, too, are foretastes of the later Mallarmé who delighted in improvising playful verse on social occasions and in rhyming on proper names: Mallarmé the poet of circumstance.

Thanks to the Dubois Davesnes, Stéphane also met the great Republican songwriter Pierre-Jean de Béranger (1780–1857), who was as legendary for the unpretentious warmth of his character as he was for the meticulous skill with which he had perfected the art of the *chanson* and raised its status in France to a level it still maintains today. For him, as for the later Mallarmé (despite appearances to the contrary), poetry was written in language that is in common use by all and thus a universal medium in which to address the fundamental concerns that each day, consciously or unconsciously, confront humankind.

On 30 October 1850 Stéphane's first stepsister, Jeanne, was born, soon to be followed by Marguerite (January 1852), Pierre (June 1853) and Marthe (September 1854). His stepbrother would eventually follow his father into the Enregistrement. A month before the arrival of Jeanne, eight-year-old Stéphane was sent to an expensive boarding-school in nearby Auteuil, which was patronized by the aristocracy and the upper bourgeoisie. It had been carefully selected by semi-aristocratic Aunt Herminie. Here he remained for two years before being moved to a college in Passy run by the Christian Brothers. It was much closer to home and undoubtedly cheaper. In his grandmother's opinion at this time Stéphane was a good-natured but idle boy, a view clearly shared by the authors of subsequent school reports. They also noted a tendency to be disruptive in class.

In the spring of 1853 the family moved to Sens, a cathedral town some 75 miles south of Paris. Numa Mallarmé had been promoted again. Having let their Boulainvilliers home the Mallarmés acquired a very large house in the centre of the town, leaving Stéphane with the Christian Brothers and Maria with her grandparents. School holidays were spent partly in Sens, partly in Passy. The idleness continued, but when Stéphane was kept down for a year he marginally increased his workrate and finally secured admission to the class above in the autumn of 1854. Meanwhile, his school reports note, the disruptive child had become withdrawn and solitary. He had no mother, and now, it seemed, he had no father or stepmother either – just the four walls of his classroom and dormitory and a handful of schoolmates, including his cousin, Anatole Rain, with whom he took his first communion on 18 June and who later became a priest.

Having moved up a class Stéphane relaxed, and hormones began to wreak their havoc. His teachers now reported on untidiness and a want of personal hygiene, later on a stubborn spirit of rebellion. Eventually he left, or was asked to leave, and resumed his education as a boarder at the Lycée de Sens in the spring of 1855. He was no happier, except during the holidays when he could go fishing with his sister Maria along the river Yonne. She was family: he felt as though he had no other. Maria was now boarding at a convent school in Paris, and he wrote to her for companionship and solace. It was as though they had both been sent to prison, while their stepbrothers and sisters enjoyed all the warmth and affection of daily life *en famille*. During the holidays, Maria, now 12, enjoyed teaching her stepsisters Jeanne and Marguerite to read and write, and after weeks in the company of their kind stepmother and her children both she and her brother felt the contrast keenly when it was time to go back to school in the autumn of 1856 – and Stéphane especially, because for the second time he was being kept down in his current class.

The following spring brought Maria's first communion, in Passy. Numa and Anna travelled up with Stéphane to join her and her grandparents at the ceremony. By way of a present her brother had already sent her his physics notes and a pressed flower. Now fifteen he was beginning to work a little harder, and at the end of the school year (10 August in those days) he came second in Greek unseen translation and fourth in French composition. As planned, he took the train to Paris the following day to go and stay with his grandparents in Passy: Maria was to follow. But on the last day of her term she fell ill. She travelled anyway, but the rheumatoid arthritis that had troubled her periodically over the preceding years (and that had probably killed her mother) now took severe hold. On 31 August 1857, at the age of thirteen, she died at her grandparents's house, 7 Grande-Rue. The shock and grief of her close relatives was no less great for the fact that such child mortality was not then uncommon.

Stéphane had lost his soulmate, his 'family'. He was virtually an orphan, like the sad and lonely boy who figures prominently in some of his early prose poems written and published during the following decade. The first version of 'L'Orgue de Barbarie' (The Barrel Organ), written in London in 1863 and later entitled 'Plainte d'automne' (Autumn Lament), begins: 'Since Maria left me on her journey to another star – oh, which one? Orion, Sirius, the Great Bear? – I have always cherished solitude.' 'La Tête' (The Head), written in Tournon in 1864 and later entitled 'Pauvre enfant pâle' (Poor Pale Child), tells of a starving street urchin, dressed in adult clothes, desperately singing his head off and clutching a little wicker basket that remains obstinately empty of alms. 'Have you ever had a father?', the observing prose-poet muses. 'You don't even have an old woman to beat you and make you forget your hunger when you come home without a sou.'

'L'Orphelin' (The Orphan), first drafted in the same year, begins: 'Orphan, already, a child of sadness with premonitions of the Poet, I was wandering, dressed in black, eyes lowered from the sky and seeking a family on the earth.' This prose poem – itself a generic hybrid and a kind of orphan – continues with an account of the child wandering round a fairground, perhaps reminiscent of the travelling circus that Aunt Herminie had taken Stéphane and Maria to see when she had visited them unexpectedly at Sens in June 1856. Each booth offers a different spectacle, sometimes a play, sometimes feats of strength, and the orphan hears and sees only other children. Already alienated from his 'hideous school-mates', he feels drawn to these vagabond performers, sensing 'a kinship' and that 'later I would be one of them'. One child wears a nightcap like 'Dante's hood', and he is eating – 'in the form of a sandwich filled with white cheese' – 'the ravished lilies, the snow, the swan feathers, the stars, and every kind of whiteness consecrated by poets.' Another child interrogates him: '"Where are your parents?" – I don't have any, I said. – "Ah, so you have no father?

I've got one."' This child is called away to play his role in a show, leaving the prose–poet to reflect: 'And I departed all alone, thinking that it was very sad that I did not have parents as he did.'

When Mallarmé later radically revised this early prose poem – the only one to which he made such wholesale changes – and published it as 'Réminiscence' in *Le Chat noir* in December 1889, the principal ingredients nevertheless remained. Some forty years after the death of his sister he still recalls an experience of orphanhood and exile in which he leaves his classmates behind and enters an alternative world of quasi-poetic performance. The child's cheese sandwich survives, but is now described as 'a superior meal'. The snow has become the 'snow of mountain peaks', while the 'ravished lilies' and the 'swan feathers' have become 'the lily or other whiteness constitutive of inner wings'. In other words, the base circumstances of a famished life have become the substance of a higher dream, of imaginary peaks to be climbed and inner flights to be flown. Poetry is a 'superior meal', a secular Eucharist for all.

Stéphane's childhood and adolescence had, unexceptionally, turned him into a solitary who sought refuge in dreams and protected his vulnerability within the four walls of a book. He began to take a greater interest in his studies, and by the end of his next year at school, in 1858, he came top of his class in English, second in French composition and Latin translation, and was runner-up for the Latin verse prize. He now entered the so-called Classe de Rhétorique, the penultimate year of study before the examination for the Baccalauréat. As was then customary, the focus during this penultimate year at school was on literature. But whereas he should have been reading his Corneille and Racine and Molière, Stéphane had discovered Romantic poetry. Lamartine, Musset and Hugo were his daily bread. And he wrote his own verse.

Aunt Herminie died at Christmas, and towards the end of February 1859 Stéphane fell seriously ill himself, with the same hereditary illness that had probably despatched his mother and certainly his sister. This was the first of his 'critical moments', and for a week his life hung in the balance. When the danger had passed, he spent a period of convalescence at home, away from his 'hideous schoolmates' and deeply immersed in the delights of his new-found poets. He may also have tasted other delights. Inside the back cover of a school notebook he recorded in secretive English: 'April 1859 – I passed a night with Emily.' Who was this Laura, this Beatrice? That April Stéphane was well enough to travel to Paris to spend some of the Easter holidays with his grandparents, and whenever he visited them now he was in the habit of spending time with younger members of some of the English and American families who owned or rented property in the neighbourhood. Emma Sullivan was one favourite, and Harriet Smythe, a seventeen-year-old blonde, was another. If 'Emily' was not in fact 'Emma', then at least three young ladies were helping him with his English. As his recent academic success showed, the classroom of flirtation was more effective than the prison of Sens.

It was also customary at school on the annual day of first communion for a chosen pupil to recite his own poem celebrating the occasion. The previous year Stéphane had tried his hand at a 'cantata', in this instance a poetic form perfected by the celebrated eighteenth-century poet Jean-Baptiste Rousseau. But his combination of twelve- and eight-syllable lines on the theme of angelic children as rivals of the heavenly hosts in praising the Almighty was not selected. This year, on the other hand, his untitled cantata on the same theme, divided into three parts ('A Mother's Prayer', 'Heaven', 'Earth') and based on a poem by Lamartine, was duly chosen. On 7 July 1859 the proud young poet read it out before the assembled school in the presence of the Archbishop of Sens, and the event was recorded in the local paper: 'The pupil Mallarmé recited a short, occasional poem that was ingeniously composed and full of brilliantly original, albeit sometimes risqué verse.' The poem does indeed demonstrate considerable technical skill, and also a hint of subversion. In the third section, the voice of the newly communicant child (an 'angel for a day') ostensibly prays on behalf of his fellow communicants that the Holy Mother shall spare their earthly mothers from the taste of gall. But his metaphor for gall – 'absinthe' – rather questionably turns this request into a plea for salvation from alcohol, or 'mother's ruin'. Soon 'the pupil Mallarmé' would be writing poems with titles like 'Six Phillis', in which an implausible plethora of mythological heroines is the excuse for a venereal pun. And he would write also of poets born of casual, sleep-inducing acts of procreation.

When he went to stay with his grandparents during the summer holidays of 1859, Stéphane was free once more: his grandfather was unwell, and Mme Desmolins was most reluctantly obliged to leave her unreliable seventeen-year-old grandson largely to his own devices. So he wrote. By way of a pilgrimage in honour of his new calling, he visited Père Lachaise cemetery and the tomb of Béranger, who had died in 1857 some six weeks before Maria. Fanny Dubois Davesnes's bust of the poet was being exhibited at that year's Salon (the annual summer exhibition at the Académie des Beaux-Arts), and Stéphane wanted to pay his own tribute via the medium into which the sculptress had initiated him. To the famous songwriter, therefore, he dedicated the first of his several 'Tombeaux', of which his subsequent 'tomb poems' in memory of Théophile Gautier, Edgar Allan Poe, Baudelaire and Verlaine are the celebrated examples. He also wrote two poems about the death of Harriet Smythe, who had died of tuberculosis that June. The tone is one of anger and religious doubt. First, his mother, then Maria, now Harriet . . . it simply beggared belief that there might be a God who loves us.

Stéphane returned to Sens to begin his final year at school, the so-called Classe de Logique. His father was seriously ill in November, and in February 1860 a major stroke left him paralysed and no longer able to work. The family bought a smart villa with a large garden on the outskirts of the old town, just as they once had in Paris, but – as in Paris – it would be a further year before the house was ready to move into. Coincidentally the Desmolins moved also, from Passy to Versailles, following André's retirement. Here they became near neighbours of the leading Romantic poet and critic Émile Deschamps, who for all his Romanticism had been a colleague of André's at the Ministry of Finance. Deschamps had moved in the circle of Victor Hugo and other leading young poets and writers in the 1830s, and he had recently been among the very first to champion Baudelaire's *Les Fleurs du mal* when that controversial collection of poems had first appeared in 1857. His library and his conversation would prove ideal classrooms for the apprentice poet.

The apprentice was now busy copying all his best poems into a notebook (the one containing his secret log of key events), and to this, his first collection of verse, he gave the title *Entre quatre murs*. For these poems, all but three of which were written in 1859, represented his poetic escapes from between the four walls of his prison-like school, and perhaps also from the confines of a highly regimented and closely policed adolescence. Paradoxically, however, they betray very little real emotion, with the notable exceptions of the poems evoking the deaths of his sister and Harriet Smythe. Rather they are experiments with form and voice, as though by learning the poet's *craft* he might one day scale those walls and join the wandering players soon to be evoked in 'The Orphan'. For the moment each poem is itself a 'classroom' – a series of stanzas, or rooms, in which the limits and possibilities of poetic expression are explored with acumen and intent.

Of the 44 texts in the collection (titles but no texts are given for a further thirteen) only two share the same poetic form. While the twelve- and eight-syllable lines so typical of the French verse tradition predominate, lines of ten syllables and of every length from seven to one syllables are also employed, and in a variety of combinations. The three standard rhyme-schemes (rhyming couplets, crossed and embraced rhymes) are all in evidence, sometimes in unusual combination. There are stanzas of every length from three to eleven lines, and one of fourteen. The young poet tries his hand at almost every known verse-form, from the ballad and the ode to the rondeau and the triolet. He orchestrates refrains and imitates dance rhythms; he flaunts contrived rhymes and relishes intricate rhyme-schemes. He makes four attempts at the sonnet, each one with a different rhyme pattern in the tercets. Experimentation is his motive, and diversity his point of honour.

As to voice, nowhere do we find the mawkish subjectivity of the self-obsessed adolescent. Rather, as with early Rimbaud, there is pastiche upon pastiche. The 1850s had been a remarkable decade in the history of French poetry, and a young poet faced a dizzying array of recent and contemporary models from which to choose. Hugo had broken a ten-year poetic silence with his *Châtiments* (1853), a vitriolic satire aimed at the Emperor Napoleon III, and then with his verse autobiography *Les Contemplations* (1856), a thematically rich and carefully structured work pivoting on the death by drowning of his newly married daughter Léopoldine in 1843. In 1859 the first instalment of Hugo's world history in verse, *La Légende des siècles*, had just appeared in the bookshops. In 1857 Lamartine had returned to form with his last great poem 'La Vigne et la maison'. Musset had died that same year, aged 46 (of the rare heart condition that bears his name), but the exoticism of his early verse (the *Contes d'Espagne et d'Italie* (1830) and the love poetry of his *Nuits* (inspired in the 1830s by his affair with George Sand) still charmed. Gautier's long-standing emphasis on poetic craftsmanship bore its most accomplished fruit in his *Émaux et camées* (1852), and the influence of this 'master' to whom Baudelaire dedicated *Les Fleurs du mal* (1857) could be seen also in Banville's playfulness (displayed in his *Odes funambulesques,* 1857) and in the emerging so-called Parnassian trend towards impassive and quasi-sacred verse exemplified by Leconte de Lisle's *Poèmes antiques* (1852). Mallarmé's *Entre quatre murs* is a sound-box echoing with their diverse voices: of the hispanophile and the orientalist, the classicist and the aesthete, the roguish youth and the grieving father, the pale loiterer and the cynical rake.

At the same time the apprentice was also copying out other people's poems, as though he were downloading his favourite tracks. Most probably taking advantage of Émile Deschamps's extensive library during the Easter holidays spent with his grandparents in Versailles and subsequently during the late summer of 1860, Stéphane filled three brown cloth-covered notebooks with some 8,000 lines of verse and entitled them *Glanes* (Gleanings). Now, as he turns eighteen, we see him radically extending his range of familiarity. Not only does he transcribe some sixteenth-century French verse (from Sainte-Beuve's pioneering anthology of 1828), he also gives prominence to two all-important new enthusiasms: the works of Baudelaire and Edgar Allan Poe. Deschamps himself was doubtless instrumental in firing these enthusiasms: because of his own for *Les Fleurs du mal*, and because of Baudelaire's for Poe. Baudelaire's first, influential essay on Poe had appeared in 1852, his version of 'The Raven' in 1853, and his translations of Poe – mostly the stories, but some further poems – were appearing regularly in periodicals. For a young poet, this was the cutting edge of his chosen art form. And like Baudelaire he began not only to transcribe Poe but to translate him – 'from the American'.

At the beginning of August, approaching the end of his last year at the Lycée de Sens, the schoolboy seemed to have maintained his academic standards: first in Latin, third in French composition, and even third in mathematics. But nowhere in English . . . And then came news that he had failed the 'Bac'. His grandmother was aghast. After a three-week break at Versailles he returned to Sens to prepare for his resit, and, despite a short period of illness, sat the exams again at the beginning of November. He passed. His reward?

An unpaid internship as assistant to a tax inspector in Sens. It was his family's dynastic wish, and he saw no way out of this particular apprenticeship. Taking stock of his life on 26 December 1860 he noted not only that he had 'passed a night with Emily' in April the previous year, and indeed that 5 July 1860 had been 'the first time I was alone with JF' (whoever she was), but that this very day, his name-day, marked a 'first step on the road to mindlessness'. An eight-to-five job, the inhibitions of living at home, and the ruthless economies imposed by his stepmother following her incapacitated husband's early retirement all represented new forms of incarceration. As adulthood beckoned, the shades of the prison-house began to close most desperately.

Salvation came in the most paradoxical of forms: a teacher. In October 1861 a new recruit to the profession arrived at his old school. Emmanuel des Essarts, a clever 22-year-old Parisian fresh out of the prestigious École Normale and horrified to be exiled to the provinces, was short, fat, myopic and camp. When excited, or reciting, or both, he was given to extravagant gesticulation of the most ridiculous kind. (Mallarmé took to calling him Signor Emmanuelcinella, as if he were Pulcinella, or Punch.) Alfred des Essarts, Emmanuel's father, had been a writer at the height of Hugolian Romanticism in the '30s, and was now head librarian at the Bibliothèque Sainte-Geneviève in the University of Paris. Through his father Emmanuel had met the cream of French literary life: Hugo, Sainte-Beuve, George Sand, Gautier and many others. Jules Michelet, France's foremost historian and a professor at the Collège de France, was a close family friend. Emmanuel himself frequented the leading salons and associated with the rising stars of Parisian literary life: Alphonse Daudet, Catulle Mendès, and the writer who was to have such a profound influence on Mallarmé's own work, the minor Breton aristocrat Auguste Villiers de l'Isle-Adam.

Like Stéphane, Emmanuel was an aspiring writer: unlike Stéphane his work had already appeared in print. Their friendship was instant, and fuelled initially by sharing the delights of the second and much expanded edition of *Les Fleurs du mal*, which had recently been published. Emmanuel was impressed by his new friend's poetic experiments and encouraged him to seek their publication. In the event Mallarmé's first publication was an anonymous theatre review, in the local newspaper *Le Sénonais*, praising the performance of 'M. Besombes and his troupe'. Two more reviews followed, equally anonymous and one of them lauding a production of Hugo's 1838 drama *Ruy Blas*. An increasingly loud note of anti-bourgeois disdain can be heard, and a somewhat ostentatious nostalgia for the days when art was truly passionate and adventurous. As he prepared to exit his teens, Mallarmé despaired of the provincial spirit of moral conformism and political reaction by which he was surrounded.

Come St Stephen's Day 1861, and after many conversations with Emmanuel, his mind was firmly made up: he was simply not cut out to be a tax inspector. Let battle commence. Father, and more especially grandfather, would have to be persuaded of the merits of his new career plan: namely, to become an English teacher and then in due course to take a degree in Modern Languages and thereafter write a doctoral thesis. From discussions with his former English master at the Lycée, as he told André Desmolins, Stéphane understood that the state was keen to make new appointments in this area. Teaching was a respectable profession which would secure him a steady income and might in time bring him every bit as much prestige as a career in the Enregistrement. He proposed that during the coming year he would remain in Sens and receive private tuition in English while he continued until June with his internship, and that thereafter he would go to spend a year in England, as a teacher of French.

Grandfather capitulated, but only after insisting (doubtless in deference to his devout wife) that in England Stéphane would teach in a Catholic school, and a boarding-school at that. His grandson

Mallarmé in 1861, aged about 19.

was outraged, and had no intention of submitting once again to such 'sequestration'. He did not insist on going to London, he told his grandmother, especially since she was so deeply apprehensive about the possible consequences of its Protestant 'freedoms': Jersey might do, even Boulogne at a pinch. Or he could live with a respectable English family . . . In the event, as we shall see, he ended up 'living in sin'. His grandmother's misgivings had not been unfounded.

As he added the travails of English grammar to the tedium of tax receipts, Stéphane continued to pursue his real career as a budding young writer. His review of Emmanuel's newly published *Poésies parisiennes* appeared in a Parisian review – under his own name, at last. Having travelled to Paris with Emmanuel to meet its editor, Olympe Audouard, Mallarmé then sent a sonnet – 'Placet' – in her honour, which duly appeared also. His first published poem, it would be faithfully retained – retitled 'Placet futile' – in his subsequent volumes of collected *Poésies* (1887 and 1899). Likewise two further poems – 'Le Guignon' (The Jinx) and 'Le Sonneur' (The Bell-ringer) – appeared in *L'Artiste* (a prestigious review that published the great Baudelaire) and would likewise be retained, the former substantially transformed.

In the two years that elapsed between school and departure for London in November 1862, Mallarmé wrote some eighteen poems that have survived. A shared admiration for Gautier's *Émaux et camées* produced the Watteauesque eroticism of 'A une petite laveuse blonde' (To a little blonde washerwoman) and the playful preciosity of 'A un poète immoral', both written for Emmanuel. But mainly he was trying his hand at that Baudelairean blend of sensuality and anguish which characterizes *Les Fleurs du mal*. The 'Tableaux parisiens', newly added by Baudelaire to the 1861 edition, inspire Mallarmé to several urban scenes: an undertaker, for example, clambering up a ladder like Romeo to defenestrate a female corpse from the bedroom of a cramped hovel, and street beggars being sadistically taunted or patronisingly advised to spend their alms not on sensible bread but on escapist tobacco, alcohol and sex. Various verse forms – Dante's onward-marching *terza rima*, Gautier's delicately tripping octosyllabic quatrain, Baudelaire's lattice-like sonnet – are employed with technical expertise in the evocation of the listless, the lascivious and the louche.

In June 1862 Mallarmé feels obliged to explain his current 'mania' for the sonnet form: 'but it is for me a great poem in miniature: the quatrains and the tercets seem to me like entire cantos, and sometimes I can spend three days getting all the parts balanced in advance, so that the whole poem may be harmonious and come close to Beauty' (*Corr.*, I. 32). Gradually Baudelairean spleen assumes a more original, Mallarméan tonality. Both 'Vere novo' and 'Tristesse d'été' (Summer Sadness) are expressions of the 'sterility' and 'impotence' that Mallarmé had experienced for some three months in the spring of 1862, when he described himself as 'this sullen individual who stands for days on end with his head on the marble mantlepiece, devoid of thought: a ridiculous Hamlet who cannot explain his low state' (*Corr.*, I. 25). Of 'Vere novo' he writes: 'this is quite a new kind of poetry, in which the material effects – of the blood, of the nerves – are analysed and blended with the moral effects of the mind and spirit, of the soul' (*Corr.*, I. 30–31). The Virgilian title (meaning 'To the New Spring') ironizes the disparity between the joy of renascent nature and the poet's wintry feelings, while for the punning wordsmith it simultaneously connotes 'new verse': once again, perhaps, a way out of loneliness and depression through art. Soon, in 'Apparition', there would also be love.

In the person of Emmanuel des Essarts the classrooms of Sens had provided the doomed apprentice tax-collector with a dual means of escape: a new career path and entrée into the literary and cultural world of Paris. And now they provided him with his life's companion. For as Stéphane stood outside the Lycée one day in spring waiting for Emmanuel, he noticed a tall, slim young woman with blue eyes and long fair hair, who had come to collect one of the pupils. This was Maria Gerhard, nanny to the three children of a well-to-do judge, M. Libéra des Presles. Maria, or Marie as she was known, was 27, and a native of Camberg in southern Germany where her widowed father was a primary school teacher. Rather plain and melancholic in appearance, she fascinated her new admirer, who was just then plunged in the gloom so keenly evoked in 'Vere novo'. He courted her energetically by word and deed. On 15 August, her name-day, he gave her some forget-me-nots. A week later he assured Emmanuel: 'Marie adores me and lives only for me. So, my worries are over' (*Corr.*, I. 48).

Marie was absent for some weeks as the Libéra des Presles holidayed in the country, but on 29 September, after her return, Stéphane took her to the forest of Fontainebleau for the day; and there in the Gorge de Franchard he asked her to accompany him to London and, by implication, to marry him. Six weeks later the lovers travelled separately to Boulogne, from whence they eloped to London's fog in early November. They rented a flat near Leicester Square and simulated married life. But for Marie the position quickly became untenable. Lonely, unable to speak English, and desperately afraid of becoming pregnant, she threatened to leave. As a sop the couple moved to Knightsbridge. But on 9 January 1863 the distraught lover was obliged to escort his unhappy mistress back across the Channel to Boulogne, from where she returned to Paris. A month later she was back, but still Stéphane procrastinated. Another month went by, and this time she left for Brussels, on 4 March.

A fortnight later Stéphane turned 21. Since the age of 18 he had been entitled to the interest on his mother's legacy – this was one thing he had learnt at the Enregistrement – but now he entered into a third of the capital, and into the whole of his sister's legacy also. The remainder would be due on the death of his father. Moreover he could now marry without the permission of his

Marie Gerhard, Mallarmé's wife-to-be, in 1862.

family. Accordingly he left for Brussels and formally proposed to Marie, reassuring her that his previous reluctance had stemmed from a fear of disinheritance.

Be that as it may, his correspondence suggests that he was now principally motivated by a sense of duty towards the woman he had 'deflowered': 'these are not just words: duty exists. . . . It would be *dishonest*, *criminal*, not to marry her. . . . I am aware of the sacrifice I am making, it is total, immense, but I *must* make it' (*Corr.*, I. 74; Mallarmé's emphases). His friends tried to dissuade him, but a still strong affection and a certain stubbornness of character prevailed over what might have been a better judgement. Loneliness had brought the two young people together, abetted by a bored young man's determination to 'have' the object of his schoolgate fantasies, but Stéphane and Marie had very little, if anything, in common. Yet this seems not to have mattered to the solitary dreamer. He had no inflated notions of romantic love, and his recent depression had doubtless made him value steady companionship the more. He may even have believed his own rhetoric: 'Two years with me, and Marie will be my reflection' (*Corr.*, I. 53). Essentially he seems to have thought that since happiness with another person was in any case a vain objective, he might as well do the decent thing: 'I would be mad to marry Marie for the sake of my own happiness. Does happiness even exist on this earth? And should one seek it – *seriously* seek it – anywhere but in dream. It is life's false goal: the true one is Duty, whether that Duty be called art, or the struggle for something, or whatever. I know full well that I shall sometimes find things very hard, and meet with major disappointments that will later torment me. . . . No, I am marrying Marie solely because without me she would not be able to live her own life, and I would have poisoned the purity of her existence' (*Corr.*, I. 87–8; Mallarmé's emphasis). Given the available role models, why would he have looked for more? Marie would be his helpmeet (and he hers) in the world of physical, material reality, just as poetry would be the guiding star to the travelling circus of his mind.

From Brussels Stéphane proceeded to Paris, where he was dispensed from military service on medical grounds, and then to Sens, where he completed the legal formalities relating to his mother's estate. He now took his understanding stepmother, who had inklings, fully into his confidence. She was to break the news of this impending and highly unsuitable marriage to her in-laws. In Paris on 11 April, on his way back to London, he was summoned back to Sens by a telegram: his father had had another very serious stroke. Had Anna told him? On the following day Numa Mallarmé died. After some ten days of practicalities but little grief for a father to whom he had never felt close, Mallarmé returned to London via Brussels: engaged to be married, and suddenly very well off, with assets of some 20,000 francs. This was 3,000 francs more than the Mallarmés had paid for their fine villa in Sens, and ten times the annual salary he would shortly earn as a schoolteacher.

The couple celebrated a Catholic wedding in the Brompton Oratory on 10 August, a ceremony duly witnessed by a respectable widow and a six-year-old choirboy. On 17 August they were back in Paris for Stéphane to sit the exams that would enable him to qualify as a teacher. By mid-September he had passed, and by early November he had been appointed to a position in the Lycée at Tournon, on the banks of the Rhone some 350 miles south of the capital. He had fondly believed that he would be teaching in or near Paris: it was quite a shock. A fortnight later his grandparents finally signed the necessary document of consent that would allow his English marriage to a German woman to be recognized under French law – and by the Enregistrement.

2

Crossroads

The next eight years in Mallarmé's life have been often discussed, not least because his surviving correspondence during this period is at its most extensive and frank. Three correspondents in particular were the poet's confidants. The most intimate was Henri Cazalis, who had been a schoolfriend of Emmanuel des Essarts in Paris. He was now studying law but in 1865 would begin training to be a doctor like his father before him – and thus become one of the models for Dr Legrandin in Proust's *À la recherche du temps perdu*. He was already a prolific (and published) poet when Mallarmé met him on 11 May 1862 and would continue to be so throughout his life.

The occasion of their meeting was a picnic in the forest of Fontainebleau, where new avenues and clearings had recently been created to welcome the day trippers now enabled by the railway to visit this beauty spot and the nearby palace. From Sens came Emmanuel, the party's organizer, and Stéphane, while from Paris came not only Cazalis but also Henri Regnault, a talented young painter; Mme Gaillard and her eighteen-year-old daughter Nina, who was a gifted poet and musician; Mrs Yapp, wife of the *Daily Telegraph*'s Paris correspondent, and two of her daughters, Ettie (Juliette), aged 17, and baby Isabelle; and Mary Green, a friend of Ettie's. This mixed party, thus properly chaperoned, took lunch in the glade known as the Carrefour des Demoiselles, a crossroads for damsels who perhaps might find themselves heading off in new directions . . . like the Path of Tender Affection or the Path of the

False Step that met at this junction. Cazalis and Ettie, for example, were clearly smitten – and would conduct an intermittent and tormented courtship until their ways parted in November 1868.

Emmanuel and Stéphane commemorated this already unforgettable occasion by creating new lyrics for a well-known song of the period. The lyrics they entitled simply 'Le Carrefour des Demoiselles', but their subtitle was keenly felt: 'The Absence of the Lancer, or the Triumph of Prudence'. Copies were specially printed and presented to the participants. That Mallarmé chose in the following September to seal his relationship with Marie with an unofficial betrothal in the forest of Fontainebleau bespoke his fond memories of this poetic gathering in the spring – and foreshadowed his later decision in 1874 to rent holiday accommodation nearby, just across the Seine at Valvins (now Vulaines-sur-Seine). In this house one of his most constant pleasures – and recurrent poetic images – would be the spectacle of a glorious blood-red sun gradually sinking down behind the trees of the ancient, seemingly timeless forest. This paradox of an unchanging cyclicity would hold him rapt, as the very emblem of the human condition: a 'play

Mallarmé's holiday home at Valvins, *c.* 1900.

written on the folio of the sky', he called it, 'and mimed by Man with the gesture of his passions' (*oc*, ii. 162). From this house the metaphysical poet of the *Poésies* would watch the solar drama, 'Nature's Tragedy' (*oc*, ii. 1461), as if from the front row of the stalls. And it was in this house that he died, suddenly, on 9 September 1898.

The picnic at Fontainebleau was thus itself a crossroads in Mallarmé's life. In particular his understanding with Cazalis was instantaneous, and in the coming months this new friend (who knew German) played a key role as intermediary and adviser in Stéphane's complex courtship with Marie Gerhard. Moreover, as Stéphane began increasingly to perceive insincerity in Emmanuel, even though he still warmed to his energy and passionate commitment to poetry, so he came to rely more and more on Henri as his closest and most trusted friend.

The second important confidant during the coming years was Eugène Lefébure. A former pupil at the Lycée de Sens, but four years older, Lefébure was currently working in the postal service at Auxerre. Later he would become a university lecturer in Egyptology in Lyons and Paris, and eventually professor in Algiers. Like Cazalis Lefébure was also an enthusiastic poet, though little of his verse would ever be published. More importantly he was the possessor of that rare thing, a copy of Poe's verse in the original. Their relationship began when Mallarmé wrote to him about this shared enthusiasm in February 1862, and they met in May, the crossroads month. A strong, intellectually rich friendship ensued.

The third confidant was another poet, Théodore Aubanel, a native of Avignon, a printer by profession, and member of the so-called Félibrige. From 'félibre', meaning 'follower' or 'pupil' in Occitan (the language of Provence), the Félibrige was an association of writers, artists and craftsmen formed in 1854 to promote Provençal culture. Emmanuel des Essarts had been transferred from Sens to Avignon in February 1863, and had lost no time in getting to know its members – nor in inviting his friend to make the 90-mile journey down the Rhone valley to meet them on several occasions during the summer. In this way Mallarmé came to know not only Aubanel but Frédéric Mistral, the most celebrated 'félibre', who later won the Nobel Prize for Literature; Joseph Roumanille, a poet and publisher, and Mistral's former teacher; and Jean Brunet, a poet and a committed socialist noted also for the beauty of his hand-blown glass and his interior decorations.

Stéphane and Marie Mallarmé arrived to begin their new life in Tournon on Sunday, 6 December 1863. Stéphane had travelled down there on 23 November to swear the customary oath on officially taking up his appointment, but he had then been obliged to make a hurried visit to the French consulate in London to complete formalities relating to the legalization of his marriage under French law. Soon after their arrival he and Marie moved into rented accommodation just opposite the school, and the young teacher settled into a grinding routine that left him feeling as 'mindless' as when he was working for the Enregistrement.

For the newly qualified professional the first year would go well enough, but by the second he was confessing to friends that the pupils heckled and threw things at him. He would arrive home with pieces of paper stuck to his back. He hated it. But it was still better than being a tax inspector, for he had a deep-seated distaste for commerce and finance. And at least he was teaching language, the poet's medium.

For the human being the first year in Tournon was difficult. Mallarmé loathed the town's climate. The bitter cold in winter and the howling Mistral wind exacerbated his rheumatic condition, while the heat in summer made life unbearable until the school holidays began in mid-August. Scorpions were a scourge, requiring bed legs to stand in bowls of water. The town had no cultural life to speak of, and the townspeople seemed to him materialistic and dull. There were no poets. Correspondence and the occasional visit of a friend were his lifelines.

After four months in Tournon Mallarmé was complaining bitterly at the tedium of his life and envying Emmanuel his ability to create excitement around him. But his own soul was 'passive, ill, weakened, powerless' (*Corr.*, I. 111), yearning for the stimulating bustle and literary gossip of Paris: 'I need people, friendly Parisiennes, paintings, music. I thirst for poets' (*Corr.*, I. 122). By day's end he is so exhausted that he goes to bed at seven. Constant sleep is his only remedy. Even to write a letter, let alone a poem, seems impossibly strenuous: 'my boredom has become a form of mental illness, and my debilitating lack of energy makes the merest task arduous.' (*Corr.*, I. 113) Home life was a refuge, and he grew apprehensive about the threat to its tranquillity on learning that Marie was pregnant: 'I tremble at the idea of becoming a father' (*Corr.*, I. 115). What, he wondered, if the child were ugly or mentally impaired?

Once the school holidays came, Mallarmé was desperate to be off, deserting Marie whose condition prevented her from travelling. After visiting Emmanuel and meeting members of the Félibrige in August, he travelled to Sens to see his stepmother and her children, and then to Versailles to stay with his grandparents. If only he could have managed London as well. But the real treat was Paris, where he immersed himself avidly once more in the world of poetry and the arts to which Emmanuel had earlier introduced him. At last he could renew former acquaintanceships: for example, with Auguste Villiers de l'Isle-Adam, who five years earlier had published his *Premières Poésies* at his own expense and had recently written a novel, *Isis*. Supported by a generous aunt, this impecunious dreamer lived a flamboyant, unconventional life and proclaimed an ardently idealist aesthetic that disdained the real and vaunted the mysterious and the bizarre. (His father had squandered his inheritance by buying up land in a quest for the buried treasure of the Knights Templar . . .) At the time Villiers was staying with Catulle Mendès, an increasingly influential young poet of the circle, whose first collection of verse *Philoméla* had appeared in 1863, and who would soon leave home to marry Théophile Gautier's younger daughter Judith in 1866. And there was Albert Glatigny, a poet Mallarmé had met through Emmanuel two years earlier and who in 1864 was just publishing his second volume of verse. He was currently working as a journalist in Vichy, as editor of *La Semaine de Cusset et de Vichy*, in which two of Mallarmé's prose poems, 'Fusain' (Charcoal Drawing; originally, The Head) and 'La Pipe' (a smoker's proto-Proustian reminiscence of London fog and cross-channel ferries), had appeared in July.

On his return to Tournon from the capital of delights the guilty poet brought his wife a beautiful mantelpiece clock made of Dresden china, to remind her of her native Germany. It became their most treasured possession. Here in Tournon, in the company of their caged birds, their goldfish and a cat called Snow, the parents-to-be awaited the birth of Geneviève. Mallarmé resumed his daily routine of teaching, and his evening and/or Sunday routine of writing. Gradually his own, original aesthetic was taking shape. The enemies were contingency and gush, of the sort that characterized the subjective lyrical outpourings of Emmanuel des Essarts: '[he] grabs a fistful of stars out of the Milky Way and strews them on the paper to form random, unforeseen constellations' (*Corr.*, I. 104). When Emmanuel's second collection of poems, *Les Élévations*, appeared at the beginning of 1865, Mallarmé wrote to Lefébure that he found them 'detestable'. The handling of rhythm was accomplished perhaps, but they were otherwise marred by sloppy thinking, clichés and an interchangeability of adjectives that signalled their vacuity. In short, they offered the reader 'no new sensation': 'I cannot stand his poetry. It goes against everything I think about this art form' (*Corr.*, I. 153).

Mallarmé himself, conversely, now insisted on the need for careful artistic control, for 'arrangement'. Hence his admiration for Villiers's prose drama, *Elën*, in which 'there is not a single syllable that hasn't been carefully weighed and reflected upon all night long' (*Corr.*, I. 154). Hence, too, his (also proto-Proustian) disagreement with Hippolyte Taine's highly influential Positivist theories about the nature of artists and writers, and which had informed his recently published *History of English Literature* (1863):

> Where I take issue with Taine is with his claim that an artist is simply a human being raised to the highest power, while I believe that one can perfectly well have a human temperament that is very distinct from one's literary temperament. . . . Taine

The 'pendule de Saxe' or Dresden china clock that Mallarmé gave to his German wife early in their married life.

sees works of art as having their source really only in impressions, and he underrates [the role of] conscious thought. Faced with a piece of paper, the artist *makes himself*. (*Corr.*, I. 154: Mallarmé's emphasis)

In this view Mallarmé was particularly influenced, as Baudelaire had been, by Poe's article on 'The Philosophy of Composition', in which the American poet had described (fictitiously, as he later admitted) the concerted manner in which his famous poem 'The Raven' had been written. Like Poe, Mallarmé's aim is not to express himself but to create an 'effect' on the reader. Of 'L'Azur', sent to Cazalis earlier that year and in which Poe's device of incantatory repetitition is particularly aped, he had written: 'I swear to you that there isn't a word in it that didn't cost me several hours of searching' (*Corr.*, I. 103). The beginning of the poem ('The serene irony of the eternal Azure . . .') introduces the main theme, he informs Cazalis, while also preparing for the 'sincere and bizarre cry of the ending' ('L'Azur! l'Azur! l'Azur! l'Azur!'). The azure sky here symbolizes the 'Idéal', a realm of spiritual coherence denied to 'the impotent poet who curses his genius / As he crosses a sterile desert of Pain' but which continues to haunt him, however much he seeks to close his eyes to it.

Though the theme is commonplace, the young Mallarmé is striving not merely to express Baudelairean spleen but to produce a stark 'effect' of anguish in his own reader. And he calls this 'effect' a 'sensation': an almost physical response, elicited by sound, rhythm and metre, such that for the reader the final line of the poem shall seem to echo endlessly into the future like the church bells mentioned in the penultimate stanza, summoning the faithful to worship. In commenting on the poems of his friends at this time, Mallarmé often couched his own response in these physical terms. Thus he compliments Lefébure the following year on the 'rare sensation' his poetry affords him: 'What dear hours I passed yesterday with your verse in my hand, breathing their delicate scent of a slightly faded rose, feeling in myself the trembling of the yellow poplars and, occasionally, those excruciating stab wounds in the spine, like sword-blades suddenly breaking . . .' (*Corr.*, I. 155).

In 'Les Fleurs', written in March 1864, the 'effect' of a flower is one of sumptuous awe at the spectacle of unfolding beauty mingled with intimations of mortality and a redemptive cyclicity. The poem opens up, like a calyx or chalice, displaying a variety of flowers in a rich sequence of imagery but seeming also to empty as it nears its final stanza. Yet just as the poem begins with the idea that flowers were originally fashioned from the gold of the sun and the snowy white-ness of the stars, so it ends with reassuring prospects of a re-creation and a resurrection: new flowers springing from the seeds released by decay, the future phial of perfume preserving a precious scent.

At the heart of this poem is the description of a rose: 'And, like woman's flesh, the cruel / rose, flowering Hérodiade of the

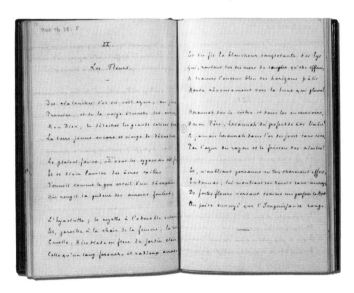

'Les Fleurs', copied out in Mallarmé's hand, 1864.

brightly-coloured garden, / Watered by a fierce and radiant blood'. This extraordinarily dense fusion of images suggests all at once a rose, soft and pink like woman's flesh, yet also crimson red as though stained with the blood spilled by its cruel thorns – and by a 'deflowering'. And there is Salome (whom Mallarmé makes more mysterious by calling her Hérodiade), veiled in petals and dancing in the breeze, perhaps even luring passers-by to bow down in search of a perfume that will cause them, like St John the Baptist, to lose their heads.

It was to this allegory of beauty that the poet returned in October 1864, his own head filled with the intoxication of a major new project that would occupy him off and on for the rest of his life: 'I have finally begun my *Hérodiade*. With terror, for I am inventing a language that must necessarily spring from a very new poetics, which I could define in these few words: *Paint not the thing but the effect it produces.*' Not the flower itself, therefore, but the quasi-religious sense of joy, mystery and fear that it may provoke. 'The line of verse must not in this instance consist of language, but of intentions, all the words must yield to the sensation.' (*Corr.* I. 137; Mallarmé's emphasis.) Words, of course, are all a poet has; but Mallarmé means that the poet must banish 'a myriad lyric graciousness' from his brain, eschew 'fine verse', and always 'remain implacably focused on his subject' (*Corr.*, I. 103). There must be no prettiness, no musical loveliness, no rhetorical self-indulgence, but rather an extreme concentration in the service of the 'effect' or 'sensation'. The 'effect' of *Hérodiade* will be one of intense and diamantine self-sufficiency and self-regard, the spellbinding, other-worldly integrity of a 'Beauty' that shuns the real in the name of an 'unknown thing'.

For Mallarmé had now found a path beyond the Baudelairean alchemy whereby the base metal of the real – the quotidian, the shoddy, the vile – is transformed by imagery and poetic form into 'flowers of evil'. Rather he is concerned to stifle narrative and description and to confound the reader who seeks to picture a real place or real event in the world. Words perforce have referents in the material world, and to speak a word is as though to utter a spell, 'evoking' or calling up dead spirits. But these words will combine to create the 'Idéal', a mental event or experience, which Mallarmé later came to call simply the *Idée* – from the Greek verb meaning 'to see', and thus a perceived form or shape. Hence he envisages Hérodiade/Salome as someone 'purely dreamt of and absolutely independent of history'. Indeed the very name 'Hérodiade' has been his inspiration: 'this word, dark and red like a pomegranate that has been split open' (*Corr.*, I. 154). Born of a word, of a name, Mallarmé's mysterious princess is a poetic construct, untouchable, non-mimetic, inhabiting a wholly imaginary domain – like the poem itself. But once again the 'effect' will be acutely physical: 'my line of verse hurts sometimes and wounds like steel'. The reader will experience sensations that are variously 'sharp, to the point of being excruciating', or 'floating', having 'the uncanny pose of a mystery' (*Corr.*, I. 161).

This is the Mallarmé of the short article entitled 'Artistic Heresies: Art for All', published in September 1862, where he rejects the notion that literature should be readily accessible and serve a public, educative function. 'Every sacred thing, and that wishes to remain sacred, wraps itself in mystery. Religions shelter behind arcane secrets that are revealed only to the chosen: art has arcane secrets of its own' (*oc*, II. 360). Poetic language is also the language of everyday intercourse, whereas musical notation, for example, is for many an impenetrable mystery that inspires reverence. The fact that words and letters serve utilitarian functions (unlike musical notation) serves to blunt readers' awareness of the non-referential, 'aesthetic' effects of poetic language. Poetry, too, must 'wrap itself in mystery'. But Mallarmé's ambition here derives not from an anti-philistine wish to prevent the common herd from being able to follow what he says, but from the belief that everyday language should be defamiliarized and its rich expressive potential thus made manifest in the very process of thwarting a utilitarian, referential reading. Any suggestion of elitism is misplaced: for 'to insult the crowd is to treat oneself as scum also', he asserts, quoting Baudelaire (*oc*, ii. 362). The purpose is a sacred, heightened form of language that may vouchsafe glimpses of the 'Idéal' to us all, intimations of that 'unknown thing' on which Hérodiade has so resolutely set her mind.

Mallarmé's work on *Hérodiade*, begun in October 1864, had been interrupted by the arrival of Geneviève on 19 November, and was resumed only in February. But, as had happened the winter before, his health was poor and his morale low. Domestic bliss, real enough, is perceived as inferior to the great 'inner felicity' granted by the Muse, and Mallarmé resents the 'hideous work of the pedagogue' that interrupts his writing (*Corr.*, i. 160). He was already planning for the summer holidays. Household expenses are mounting, and he wonders even about taking up the suggestion of one of Cazalis's acquaintances that he give a course of twelve lectures on French Romantic poetry in Switzerland that summer. But August seemed distant. Once again he felt that this solitude was ill-advised for a 'weak head' like his: rather he needed 'every conceivable stimulus, to be fired by the voice of friends, paintings, music, the noise of life' (*Corr.*, i. 150). Where he had once boasted to Cazalis of a future compatibility with his wife, now that compatibility was the tedium of Narcissus: 'you will tell me that I have Marie; but Marie is me, and I see my own reflection in her German eyes.' And baby Geneviève? 'It is lovely to cuddle her for ten minutes, but then?'(*Corr.*, i. 151) After a long day in the classroom the evening he had been looking forward to – 'Jacob's holy hour, the struggle with the Ideal' – is a purgatory of blank exhaustion. He apologizes to Cazalis for moaning, but . . .: 'a poor poet, who is only a poet – that is to say, an instrument that resonates beneath the fingers of his diverse sensations – is mute when he lives in a milieu where nothing stimulates him; his strings slacken, and then comes dust and oblivion'.

This image of the poet-instrument informs two important texts. One is the prose poem originally entitled 'La Pénultième' (later 'Le Démon de l'analogie'), which Mallarmé may have begun at this period even though he sent it to Villiers de l'Isle-Adam only in 1867 (with a view to publication). Here, in a story reminiscent of Poe's 'The Imp of Perversity', the poet fantasises about leaving his apartment one day 'with the real sensation of a wing brushing lightly across the strings of an instrument'. This sensation is then 'replaced by a voice speaking the words "The Penult is dead" as a falling cadence, with the result that "The Penult" finished the line and "Is dead" detached itself from the fateful suspension more blankly still in the emptiness of signification' (*oc*, I. 416–17). Since the penult in French is 'Pénultième' and in both languages means the penultimate syllable of a line of verse, the prose poem narrates how the poet is seized by a linguistic and prosodic possibility – and one so much more interesting than the 'linguistic labour' by which the 'noble poetic faculty' of this English teacher is daily interrupted. For the enjambment necessary to turn the word 'nul' (null, none) into the penult itself has thus been dictated to the poet by some mysterious 'voice', rendering the word 'pénultième' newly expressive – as the prose poem goes on to relate – like a forgotten musical instrument whose strings have been tautened and tuned.

The poet then walks through the streets mentally rehearsing the mysterious phrase, allowing the words to play randomly across his lips until magically his own voice coincides with the mysterious voice he had originally heard. And at this moment of coincidence he perceives his hand, reflected in a shop-window, gradually falling in a gesture of caress across some object or other. On further examination he realizes that his footsteps have led him to a street full of antique shops and that he is now standing in front of one such shop in which old musical instruments hang on the wall, and the floor is littered with yellowing palm leaves and the feathered wings of birds – which provide writers with their quill pens. A random phrase, haunting him like a ghost, has provoked the poet-musician into a linguistic performance that miraculously confronts him with the antique shop of word-instruments, created long ago by a luthier and still waiting to be plucked.

The second important text in which this image occurs is the short, perfectly symmetrical poem of four octosyllabic quatrains that Mallarmé sent to Mme Cécile Brunet in December 1865. The wife of Jean Brunet, the Félibrige craftsman known also for his glasswork, Cécile had stood in for Mme Desmolins as Geneviève's godmother at her christening and had recently celebrated her name-day on 22 November, the feast-day of St Cecilia, patron saint of music. As would later become customary for Mallarmé, these chance circumstances prompt a display of poetic necessity. Entitled 'Saint Cecilia playing on the wing of a cherubim' (later shortened, in the French, to 'Sainte'), this exquisite poem simulates a stained-glass window in which the saint, a 'musician of silence', sits with her finger delicately poised over the cherubim's harp-like wing. To one side, as though rejected, lie an old viola, its sandalwood fading and its gilt decoration almost flaked away, and also a text and/or score of the Magnificat, opened wide but unread and unperformed. The implication is that a new form of poetry – a secular orchestration of suggestive silence, exemplified by the poem itself – is better able to evoke the sacred mysteries than the open book of Christian ritual.

'Sainte' offers an intricate latticework of verbal echoes and parallels that anticipates Mallarmé's later equation of music with the *Idée*, in turn defined as 'rhythm between relationships' (*Corr.*, VI. 26). This conception of poetry as a form of 'relational music' had been evolving during his work on *Hérodiade* during the previous spring, but in June 1865 he set *Hérodiade* aside – 'for the cruel winters' – and embarked instead on a poem about a faun, the horned woodland creature of Roman mythology, half-human, half-goat, and follower of Bacchus, god of wine. 'This poem', he tells Cazalis, 'contains a very lofty and very beautiful idea, but the verse is terribly difficult to do, because I want it to be absolutely scenic, not just *possible in the theatre* but *absolutely demanding the theatre*' (*Corr.*, i. 166; Mallarmé's emphases). Mindful of the popularity of Théodore Banville's one-act verse-dramas on mythological subjects, Mallarmé is thinking of offering it to the Comédie-Française in August while he is in Paris.

Mallarmé's conceptions of poetry as having an 'effect' on the reader and as being a form of 'relational music' also underlie this new project, and, as he tells Lefébure in July, he is particularly preoccupied by the need to synchronize the rhythms of his verse with the gestures that an actor might potentially make in further expression of its meaning. At the same time he is becoming increasingly conscious of the importance of homophony in his drive towards a quasi-musical poetry that defamiliarizes and reinvigorates the potential meanings of words. Terminal rhyme in particular – for Mallarmé, as for Banville, the foundation-stone of poetry – draws attention to the different meanings of same-sounding words and thereby reveals a supplementary network of meanings to which we are blinded (and deafened) by the incontro-vertibility of print. In a theatre, on the other hand, we can but listen to these plural possibilities and thus be subjected to the enrichment of ambiguity. In French 'Faune' is a faun, but also homophonically (in the pronunciation of the time) a 'phone', or 'unit of sound'. A poem that was eventually entitled *L'Après-midi d'un faune* thus begins to sound like a poem about language struggling, in the aftermath of a midday vision, to express what has been witnessed. If Hérodiade symbolizes the self-sufficient, non-mimetic realm of poetic beauty and the *Idée*, then perhaps this Faun figures the poetic voice in its pursuit of beauty.

The projected work was to be an 'intermezzo', or 'entr'acte', a play performed either in the interval of another play or else between two short plays. It is itself about interruption. This so-called 'Intermède héroïque' was to be comprised of three parts:

the Faun's waking monologues ('Monologue of a Faun', 'The Faun Awakes') before and after his dream of two nymphs conversing ('Scene between Iane and Ianthé'). But when the work was rejected by Banville and Coquelin, the director of the Comédie-Française, on the grounds that it lacked sufficient plot even for a one-act drama, Mallarmé later fused the three parts into one single monologue. The Faun believes that he has espied two nymphs through the bushes and seeks to recover this climactic, midday vision of beauty: at first by evoking the nymphs on his reed-pipes (consisting here of two conjoined pipes), only for his music to prove too insubstantial ('A sonorous, vain and monotonous line'); and then by representing the nymphs drunkenly and quasi-pictorially in words that constitute a form of violation serving only to chase them away. The poem itself by contrast steers an emblematic middle path between music and narrative, subtly 'perpetuating' these nymphs in dense, richly orchestrated verse that derives as much of its suspense from the tension between syntax and metre as from the elusiveness of the Faun's glimpses of the 'Idéal'.

The reflexive character of what Mallarmé was trying to do here is suggested by a comment to Cazalis in July 1865, which shows the poet confronting this very issue: 'How hard you have to study the sound and colour of the words, the music and painting which your thought – however fine – has to pass through for it to be poetic' (*Corr.*, I. 168). The poem thus – at this early stage as much as in its final published version of 1876 – can be read as an allegory of the tension that lies at the heart of all poetry and indeed of rhyme itself, the dialectic of sound and sense. On the one hand, the two nymphs are initially locked in such a close embrace (like the reed-pipes) that they are indistinguishable one from the other: rhyme is mere repetition, 'monotonous' sonority empty of the differentiation on which meaning depends. On the other, the Faun sunders the couple crudely as though in an act of penetrative 'deflowering', only to find that like-sounding 'Iane' and 'Ianthé' (in the original version) part company, lose connection, escape entirely, as in a surfeit of difference. Like the Faun the poetic act is half human, half goat: spiritual in its imaginary pursuit of the 'Idéal', goat-like in its base referential capture of the real by naming rather than suggesting.

After a September trip to Paris via Sens and Versailles the school-teacher-poet returned to Tournon, where the Mallarmés moved into a small house with a wonderful view of the river (and the sunset) and some much-needed space for their growing collection of birds, cats and antiques, notably a lovely Venetian mirror. Newly rein-vigorated the poet resumed work on *Hérodiade*, 'no longer as a tragedy [because, like his Faun poem, it lacked plot] but as a poem' (*Corr.*, I. 174). In mid-December, just as Lefébure had come to stay, Mallarmé's grandfather André Desmolins died. Mallarmé despatched Lefébure down the Rhone to Avignon and the hospitality of Aubanel, while he himself travelled up to Versailles to comfort his grandmother, who was already finding solace in her faith. Having dealt with the practicalities and on the point of making it back to Tournon in time for Christmas (Geneviève's second), he found himself invited to a splendid New Year's Eve party to be presided over by Leconte de Lisle, who was perhaps (given Hugo's exile on Guernsey) the most actively influential poet of the moment. Coincidentally or mendaciously Mallarmé found he had a boil on his bottom: travel would be impossibly painful in the coming days.

On his return all vestiges of gloom had lifted, dispersed by his receipt in Paris of 'the most cordial and most triumphal welcome for a Poet you could possibly imagine' (*Corr.*, I. 186). He had made new poet-friends, notably François Coppée, and also José-Maria de Heredia. The latter gave him a copy of his sonnets and a repro-duction of Titian's painting of Salome, which he hung on his wall. As Mallarmé told Mistral in his New Year's Day letter of greeting: 'spleen has almost deserted me, and my poetry has raised itself up on its ruins, tinged with its enriching shades of cruel solitude, but luminous. I have overcome my sense of artistic impotence, and my soul moves freely' (*Corr.*, I. 190).

1866 marked the beginning of a period of crisis for Mallarmé, and yet in many respects it seemed like a very good year. Money, admittedly, was short. His grandmother, in any case now subject to a widow's straitened circumstances, was sparing with her gifts and loans: she was keen to honour her husband's memory and advice by preventing their grandson from frittering his future inheritance away (for example, on expensive travel and a taste for antiques). In January/February, again his low months, Mallarmé also fell quite seriously ill with a chest infection that continued to worry him until the summer, and he continued to rail against the teaching: 'What jobs our society inflicts on its Poets!' (*Corr.*, I. 233). But in his work on *Hérodiade* the poet felt a new sense of momentum and sustained, purposeful continuity. An Easter visit to Lefébure's

Geneviève Mallarmé in 1866, aged about 2.

new home in Cannes proved a tonic. Although lack of funds had prevented Marie and 'Vève' from accompanying Mallarmé on this visit, some limited success at the casino in Monte Carlo at least permitted the egotist to buy his family some presents.

The poets in whose company Mallarmé had seen in the New Year under the aegis of Leconte de Lisle were preparing to publish their work as a weekly review, to be called *Le Parnasse contemporain* (in honour of the mountain home of the nine muses) and to be edited by Catulle Mendès and Xavier de Ricard. Mendès invited Mallarmé to contribute. Individual poets were to be featured, alone or in small groups, in eighteen instalments from Saturday, 3 March onwards. Mallarmé sent thirteen poems, of which ten appeared on 12 May.

At the end of April Mallarmé told Cazalis proudly of the progress he had made with *Hérodiade*. So far he had been working on a 'scene' between the eponymous princess and her former nurse in which Hérodiade shuns the physical world, symbolized by this woman who once gave her suck. In the first half of the scene – a poem of alexandrines (twelve-syllable lines) arranged in rhyming couplets in dialogue form – the nurse makes three physical approaches towards Hérodiade, as though she would understand the nature of her beauty better, and each time she is rejected. Wistfully the nurse imagines giving herself to Hérodiade's future husband in order to have a description of her former infant's 'charms'. In the second half this untouchable yet nubile emblem of beauty disdains the prospect of defiling union with a mortal male and anticipates instead some higher form of encounter with an 'unknown thing': not death but that which lies beyond it, her 'eternal sister', the 'mystery' of beauty itself (which the nurse so crudely wishes to have revealed). The poem thus allegorizes poetic aspiration as a withdrawal from referential reality towards the ineffable secret of 'mystery'. And though at this stage in the project 'the head of St John' figures only in the dramatis personae (on the extant manuscript), Mallarmé is already envisaging St John the Baptist as the key intermediary. As she stands at this crossroads in her life, Hérodiade concludes, while gazing at herself in a mirror and asking 'Am I beautiful?', that beauty requires a beholder if it is to exist at all, if virginity is not simply to be a form of sterility. What better answer to her dilemma than an observing head severed from its desiring body, registering her perfection with its eyes but unable with its lips to divulge and perhaps defame the secret of this perfection?

Now, as Mallarmé tells Cazalis in April 1866, he is drafting a 'musical overture' to this scene, whose 'effect' will be extraordinarily powerful and 'unheard of'. Indeed it will be literally 'unheard of' since, whereas the 'Scène' relies heavily on narrative and imagery, this poem shows Mallarmé manipulating homophonic patterns in an extraordinarily complex manner, and one that demands a new form of 'aural' reading that its readers would have been (and remain) quite unused to conducting. The 96 alexandrines of this poem pivot on the single verb 'S'élève' (rises) so that the whole represents the rise and fall of a voice: the voice of the nurse, herself now envisaged as a sibyl, seeking in a form of incantation to call up the 'scene' that will follow. Here the allegory represents the voice of language casting off old procedures of naive reference and engaging rather in a process of phonetic and semantic dissemination. 'Hérodiade', evoking the French words *héraut* (herald), *Éros* and *dyade*, proclaims the advent of a new kind of poetry made of quasi-erotic, dyadic couplings, of sounds, rhymes, couplets, synonyms and antonyms that almost – but not quite – defy comprehension.

Later, in December, Mallarmé would tell Coppée exactly what he envisaged: 'what we [poets] must aim for especially in a poem is for the words – which are already sufficiently themselves not to take on any further colouring from outside the poem – *to bounce reflections off one another to the point where they seem no longer to have a colour of their own but rather to be simply transitions from one musical key into another*' (*Corr.*, I. 234: Mallarmé's emphasis). One notes again, as in *L'Après-midi d'un faune*, the combination of the pictorial and the musical, the seen and the heard. But for the moment Mallarmé simply told Cazalis that even if it were to take him another 'three or four winters' to complete *Hérodiade*, he would at last have written something worthy of Poe. And he acknowledged his new-found optimism: 'that I can speak to you with such confidence, I the eternal victim of discouragement, just shows you that I must be able to glimpse real splendours!' (*Corr.*, I. 207) .

He then confides, in this letter which is explicitly intended to bring Cazalis up-to-date on how he has been over the past three months, that 'unfortunately, in digging down into verse like this, I have encountered two chasms, and they make me despair [*qui me désespèrent*]'. Yet the tone of this letter is far from being one of anguish or depression, and by 'désespérer' Mallarmé means rather 'deprive me of hope' – hope of a life hereafter, and hope of a long life in the here and now. He explains what he means: 'One [chasm] is Nothingness [le Néant], which I came to without knowing about Buddhism.' Lefébure was well-informed about Buddhism, and the most plausible inference is that the two men had discussed these matters at Easter and again just recently during Lefébure's two-week stay in Tournon. Mallarmé then elaborates on his own conception of 'Nothingness':

Yes, *I now know for a fact*, we are just pointless forms of matter, and yet thoroughly sublime ones for having invented God and our soul. So sublime, my friend! that I intend to treat myself to this spectacle of matter – of matter wholly conscious of being just matter and yet crazily launching itself into the world of Dream that it knows does not exist – singing of the Soul and all the other impressions of the divine that have accumulated in us since earliest times and proclaiming these glorious lies in the face of the Nothing [*le Rien*] that is the real truth! Such is the plan for my volume of lyric verse, and such perhaps shall be its title: *The Glory of the Lie*, or *The Glorious Lie*. I shall sing as a man who is without hope [*en désespéré*]!

Mallarmé had long since, and much to his grandmother's sad displeasure, 'lapsed' from the Catholic faith in which he had been brought up. But here he consciously and indeed happily adopts a thorough-going atheist position as the future basis for his poetry.

The other 'chasm' is his chest. He genuinely fears that he may not have long to live, and this exacerbates his impatience at having to earn a living in order to support his wife and child. Eventually, in August, he sought – and received – assurance from a homeopathic doctor in Avignon that his lungs were not affected. He was spared, for now. But, said the doctor, he should be wary of the nervous exhaustion brought on by working at his poetry into the small hours of the night – and when he had usually to be in class at eight o'clock the next morning. It was this exhaustion indeed that had made the Easter visit to the Côte d'Azur so welcome.

Following his April profession of faith in poetry and in the validity of writing against the backdrop of what the Existentialists would later call the Absurd, Mallarmé tried once more to set aside his winter poem, *Hérodiade,* in order to concentrate on his summer poem about the Faun. But his preoccupation with the former was growing: 'I dream of it being so perfect that I don't even know if it will ever exist' (*Corr.*, I. 213). The thirteen poems he had just tidied up and sent to Mendès demonstrated to him how far and how fast his poetic art had now developed into something truly original, and, as Cazalis learnt in May, his ambitions were becoming even more grandiose: 'I am in the process of laying the foundations of a book on the *Beautiful. My spirit moves in the Eternal, and feels several of its tremors* – that is, if one can talk about the Immutable like that . . . I shall continue my study of aesthetics, which will lead me to the greatest book ever written on Poetry.' At the same time he is 'relaxing' by working on 'three short poems' ('but which will be unheard of, all three a glorification of Beauty') and also 'an equal number of singular prose poems'. 'Such will be my summer', he announces, with clear delight (*Corr.*, I. 216–17: Mallarmé's emphases).

In July Mallarmé updated Cazalis further: 'for a month now I have been among the purest glaciers of Aesthetics . . . having discovered Nothingness, I have found the Beautiful' (*Corr.*, I. 220). And he takes Aubanel, too, into his confidence:

> I have laid the foundations of a magnificent work. Every man has a Secret in him, many die without ever finding it, and never will because they are dead, so it will no longer exist, just as they no longer exist. I am dead, and resuscitated with the jewelled key to the ultimate casket of my mind and spirit. I must now open it, in the absence of all borrowed impressions, and its mystery will flow forth under the most beautiful sky. (*Corr.*, I. 222)

When Aubanel, understandably, asked for clarification, it came in this form:

> I simply wanted to tell you that I had just drafted the plan of my entire work, after having found the key to myself, the keystone – or centre, if you prefer, to avoid mixing metaphors – the centre of myself, where I sit like a sacred spider on the principal threads that have already spun out from my mind and with which I shall weave, *where they cross*, some marvellous lacework that I begin to discern, and which exists already within the breast of Beauty. (*Corr.*, I. 224–5; Mallarmé's emphasis)

In these two statements we have the first glimmerings of the 'Great Work', or the Book, that Mallarmé would allude to periodically throughout the remainder of his life but which would also keep changing in both tenor and projected structure. Here he mentions 'the five books of which the work will be composed', and a period of twenty years in which he would write it. Some ten days later, in response to a further plea for clarification from Aubanel, he defines his '*œuvre*' as 'the totality of literary works that together constitute the poetic existence of the Dreamer' (*Corr.*, I. 226). He has come to the view that poetry is a criss-cross of linguistic elements, a 'centre' from which the poet, god-like, creates a 'web' of sound and meaning having a coherence and logic of its own. The lyric poem is not so much a reflection of the world (of nature, say, or of subjective feeling) as a world in itself, an event. The ambition now is to create a parallel universe of such 'worlds' or 'events', having a 'beauty' of pattern to fill the void of 'Nothingness'.

The progress that Mallarmé was making with his poetic art was in inverse proportion to his success as a teacher. The school had been inspected in May, and the inspector's report on the 24-year-old poet was uncompromising. Monsieur Mallarmé, it seems, had been sharing his exciting poetic discoveries with his nonplussed and unruly pupils. There was little or no method in his teaching, and he was neglecting practical language work. Cultivated he might be, but his manner was superior and pretentious. And it was not just the school inspector: even Aubanel and Mendès were losing patience with their friend's obscurity. But the alleged 'pretentiousness' concealed a very real – though as yet not maturely articulated – originality: and perhaps even the foundations of Modernism.

His time was up: the headmaster pretended that he needed to economize by having someone who could teach both English and German (which Mallarmé never mastered, even for pillow talk), but it was nonetheless clear that this would be his last year in Tournon. Moreover there was growing unrest among the parents, some of whom had read – or heard about – the poems that this bizarre man had recently published. Accordingly Mallarmé mobilized what influence he could exert in high places to be posted north to his old school in Sens, where there was a vacancy. But in the event he was sent east, to Besançon, on the southern edge of the Jura mountains. It might be Victor Hugo's birthplace, but it was still a long way from Paris and, even worse, a long way from his friends in Avignon.

One can therefore imagine Mallarmé's delight when two packages arrived at his new address towards the end of 1866. One, from Coppée, contained his collection of verse entitled *Le Reliquaire*, and Mallarmé wrote to compliment its young 'Parnassian' author on the 'purity' of his work in which no single word – 'and that's the great thing' – had been left to chance (*Corr.*, I. 234). The other package was from Paul Verlaine: it contained a copy of his first, pioneering collection of poems, the *Poèmes saturniens*, newly published. The two men had never met, but this was the beginning of a famous friendship that spanned the next three decades. Mallarmé praised Verlaine for the originality of his poetic technique. It almost made him regret his 'vanity', he said, in having now firmly decided not to publish any of his own work until it was all quite perfect – 'after which I shall be fit for nothing save only for my own decline' (*Corr.*, I. 236). The Monte Carlo gambler was now conscious of playing for the highest stakes – on a single throw of the dice.

3

Chasms

The Mallarmés arrived in Besançon in early November 1866 and moved into rented accommodation near the Lycée. It was still in the process of being refurbished, but the location would be convenient for those 8 a.m. starts. More than two months passed before they felt they could call the place their own. On 20 December Mallarmé wrote to Armand Renaud, a civil servant and a former poet-protégé of Émile Deschamps. Renaud, whom he had known for some three years, had pulled strings to secure this new posting for the disgraced teacher, and his grateful friend had hung a picture of him on the wall of his new home. He now tells the poet-bureaucrat of his progress with the 'Great Work':

> I worked infinitely hard this last summer, on myself first of all, by creating, in the most beautiful synthesis, a world in which I am God – and on a Work that will result from it, a pure and magnificent Work, I hope. I haven't abandoned *Hérodiade*, on the contrary I'm actually spending more time on it. It will be one of the splendid, twisting, Solomonic columns of this Temple. I am giving myself twenty years in which to complete it, and the rest of my life will be devoted to an Aesthetics of Poetry. My outline plan is complete, I've just got to find the right position for certain poems within it – their appointed, mathematical place. My entire life has its *idea*, and every minute at my disposal is directed towards it. I intend to publish

the whole thing in one block, and to detach fragments of it beforehand only for my closest friends, like you, my dear Armand. (*Corr.*, XI. 21–2; Mallarmé's emphasis)

'My entire life has its *idea*': having already taken the decision to devote his life to poetry, Mallarmé was now committing himself to a particular, all-encompassing poetic masterpiece in which *Hérodiade* had become but one single, albeit highly important, element. Building on Poe's doctrine of beauty as an 'effect', mindful of the quasi-physical 'sensation' that poetry must provoke in its readers, confident of the viability of the 'Glorious Lie' in a material world devoid of transcendent meaning or purpose, and increasingly adept at producing 'relational music' – the *Idée* – with the sounds and semantics of the French language, Mallarmé appears here to be entering with Masonic solemnity into proud possession of his own unique poetic project. The tone is assured and sincere, fearing no ridicule.

Only in a remarkably overwrought letter to Cazalis written the following May (*Corr.*, I. 240–44) do we first discover at what cost this assurance has been won, and on what fragile foundations it rests. 'I have just spent a terrifying year', he declares to his closest friend: 'my Thought has thought itself, and has arrived at a pure Conception.' Mallarmé describes himself as being 'perfectly dead', after a 'long agony' of 'unrecountable' suffering: 'the impurest region into which my Mind can venture now is Eternity itself, my Mind, this habitual solitary of its own Purity, on which Time itself can no longer cast its shadow.' Where once he had looked forward to writing in the evenings – 'Jacob's holy hour struggling with the Ideal' – here he talks of 'my terrible struggle with that wicked old plumage – now fortunately laid out cold – God'. But God, like Jacob's Angel, has put up a surprisingly 'vigorous' fight, and his 'bony wing' has sent the poet flying through the darkness, wherein he falls 'victorious' to earth: 'until one day I saw myself again in my Venetian mirror, the person I had forgotten I was some several months before'.

He confesses to Cazalis – 'but to you alone' (since others might fear for his sanity?) – that he still needs to look at himself in this mirror in order to be able to think: 'otherwise I would become Nothingness once more'. 'This tells you', he explains, 'that I am now no longer a person, no longer the Stéphane you have known – but a means by which the spiritual Universe can see and unfold itself through what was once me.' 'Fragile', like some 'terrestrial apparition', he can but submit himself to these unfoldings, which are 'absolutely necessary if the Universe is to recover its identity in this new me': 'identity', that is to say, its identicalness, its sameness, its coherence. This coherence he again calls a 'Synthesis' (as he had to Renaud), and he tells Cazalis how he now plans to structure 'the work that will be the image of this unfolding': 'three verse poems, of which *Hérodiade* will be the Overture, but of a purity that no man has ever achieved and perhaps ever will, for it is quite possible that I have been the plaything of some illusion and that the human machine is insufficiently developed to produce such results. And four prose poems, about the process of conceiving mentally and spiritually of Nothingness.'

At issue here is the 'parallel universe' of his poetic construct in which the multiple interconnections inherent in langage are further woven by the poet, not to communicate a feeling or a supposedly pre-existing thought but, as it were, to let language speak more richly for itself. Indeed thought is possible only in language (Mallarmé believes), and so the application of the art of 'relational music' to language engenders new 'thoughts' – 'Idées' – of greater complexity and eloquence. As a consequence of this multiplication of reference, the mind takes leave of a real world reassuringly mapped by narrative and description from within a stable subjectivity and enters rather into an impersonal mental space where words spin vertiginous, never-ending webs of entrancing, lace-like pattern.

Much later Mallarmé would write calmly of the poet 'ceding the initiative to words' (*OC*, II. 211), implying that the initiative can be seized back at any time by the poet-in-command. But here, at the outset of the Mallarméan adventure, it is clear that Stéphane's struggle with the Angel has had far-reaching effects on his own mental stability. There is no God, no guarantee of meaning or order in a chaotic world, only patterns wrought by language. He feels out of his depth, unable to touch bottom.

He concludes this letter by telling Cazalis that he has made 'a sufficiently long journey down into Nothingness to be able to speak with certainty. There is only Beauty – and there is only one perfect way of expressing Beauty, and that is Poetry.' By 'Beauty' he means the pleasing and ontologically consoling 'effect' of pattern. If he asserts the supremacy of poetry – in implicit but probably conscious opposition to Hegel's (and Wagner's) contention that music is the supreme art form – it is because in seeking to pattern the world poetic language can steer a middle path (as *L'Après-midi d'un faune* demonstrates) between the semantic vacuity of music and the crass explicitness of pictorial representation. 'Everything else is a lie', he proclaims: 'except love, for those who live by the body, and the spiritual form of love that is friendship.' Here he is alluding to Cazalis's own continuing relationship with Ettie Yapp, and of course to their own friendship. But he is also implying to his friend – who had once advised him strongly not to marry Marie – that he was perhaps right. 'Since you are happy enough to be able to have love as well as Poetry, then love [her] . . . For me, Poetry takes the place of love because poetry is in love with itself and its voluptuous self-attraction reflects back deliciously into my soul.' This indeed was the poet who had told Lefébure two years earlier that he could not use the word 'love' in poetry 'without smiling' (*Corr.*, I, 155).

This remarkable letter affords key insights into Mallarmé at this critical moment in his life, into his aesthetics and into the reality of his private life. Only poetry truly matters to him: 'the Poet has his Thought for a wife, and his Poetry for a child'. He believes, rightly, that he has evolved a radically new conception of poetry that calls everything – God, knowledge, personal identity – into question. So convinced is he of the value of this 'ultimate casket' that the entirely plausible prospect of a premature death torments him: 'I need ten years: will I have them? . . . I confess that the knowledge I have acquired, or rediscovered in the depths of the man I was, would not in itself suffice for me, and that I would suffer very real pangs of regret if I were to enter into the supreme Disappearance without completing my work, which is *The Work*, the "Great Work" as our ancestors the alchemists used to say.'

This apparent paradox of a willingly embraced death of self accompanied by a real fear of physical demise is echoed in another important letter, which Mallarmé wrote to Lefébure some two weeks later (*Corr.*, I. 244–7). On the previous day, a time-rich Sunday, he had 'completed the first outline plan of the work, perfectly set out and imperishable as long as I myself don't perish'. He sees this work as an explicitly post-Christian embodiment of Beauty. 'The *Venus de Milo* [and] da Vinci's *Mona Lisa*', he writes, 'seem to me – are – the two great scintillating manifestations of Beauty on this earth – and this Work, as envisaged in my dreams, is the third.' The *Venus de Milo*, he says, exhibits 'Beauty [that is] complete and unconscious, unique and immutable', while the *Mona Lisa* exemplifies 'Beauty having, since the advent of Christianity, been bitten in the heart by the Chimera, and painfully returning to life with a smile full of mystery, but a forced smile and one which it *feels* as the very condition of its being.' And then there is Mallarmé's Beauty, which

> through human knowledge has rediscovered its *correlative phases* in the Universe at large, is in possession of Beauty's final word as it recalls the secret horror that once forced it

to smile – in da Vinci's day, and to smile mysteriously –
and now still smiling mysteriously, but with happiness and
having rediscovered the eternal quietude of the *Venus de Milo* –
having gained an intellectual grasp of that mystery which the
Mona Lisa experienced only as fateful sensation. [Mallarmé's
emphasis]

The terms in which Mallarmé here makes such an ambitious
claim for his own work are quite different from his comments
to Cazalis and must be understood against the largely inaudible
background of his ongoing discussions with Lefébure. Indeed
their apparent pretension derives from the certain knowledge
that his correspondent would understand his terms of reference.
In the company of this aspirant Egyptologist Mallarmé had discovered not only Buddhism but some of the latest ideas about
the nature of religion and mythology.

In his account of the three ages of Beauty Mallarmé is suggesting
that by promoting a (chimerical) belief in a potentially paradisal
afterlife and the possibility of individual resurrection (as opposed
to the more general metempsychosis of Buddhism) Christianity
has placed existential dissatisfaction necessarily at the heart of
human experience. The smile of the *Mona Lisa* bespeaks at once
the melancholic recognition of a terrestrial inadequacy and the
anguished contemplation of a mysterious perfection beyond death.
For Mallarmé 'modern' beauty will marry the self-sufficiency of
ancient beauty – its untroubled confidence in the intrinsic value
of pattern and symmetry within the here and now – and a new,
open-eyed awareness of the contingency of a godless universe and
the absence of any transcendental 'explanation'. At the same time
this new form of beauty will be attuned to the 'correlative phases'
of the Universe, which Mallarmé will later call the 'pure rhythmic
motifs of being' (*oc*, ii. 294): for example, the diurnal and annual
passages of the sun, which, for all their ultimate inexplicability,

structure time with the cyclical rhythms of rising and setting, of the seasons, of birth, death and rebirth, and thereby offer the solace of order amidst chaos.

This 'solar drama' was central to the most innovative thinking about mythology and comparative religion at this period, notably in the writing of Friedrich Max Müller, and it is reasonable to conjecture that Mallarmé had encountered these ideas initially through Lefébure. Müller, a Sanskrit scholar and expert in comparative philology at Oxford, argued that all myths and religions derived from one original myth about the solar passage, a symbolic pattern that allowed the primitive mind to inscribe the fact of individual human mortality within a broader context of eternity and endless renewal. The apparent divergence of myths and religions was simply evidence of linguistic 'disease': as human beings had spread out across the globe, the original story and the original mythological names had gradually become distorted as in a game of Chinese whispers. For Mallarmé this thesis – and in particular the centrality of language in myth-making – became the linchpin of his thinking about poetry in a post-Christian context.

He had also been reading an article in the latest edition of the *Revue des Deux Mondes*, by Émile Montégut, in which this influential commentator argued that the modern poet was above all a *critic*. The article struck a chord with Mallarmé, who shared his thoughts with Lefébure:

> That's exactly what I observe in myself – I have created my work only by *elimination*, and each truth won has derived simply from the loss of an impression, which, having once flared, then burnt itself out and allowed me – these particular forms of darkness thus removed from my path – to advance more deeply into the sensation of absolute Darkness. Destruction was my Beatrice. (*Corr*., I. 245–6)

Just as Beatrice acts as Dante's guide through paradise in *The Divine Comedy*, so the principle of elimination has governed the poet as he distilled his poetry into a purely linguistic construct by suppressing all obfuscating reference to his subjective impressions of real things, real people and real events. The latent parallel here with Buddhist meditation, whereby all links with the real world are gradually stripped away, is significant. Three weeks earlier Lefébure had written to sympathize with his friend in his feeling of 'discouragement', recognizing the heavy demands placed upon him by climate and classroom and by his 'relations with the Muse', and predicting imminent recovery 'after some time of thought-free rest, a perfect Nirvana of the brain' (*Corr.*, I. 247, n. 1). But in his own letter Mallarmé denies all ability to arrive at his conception of 'Nothingness' by willed, intellectual means and confesses rather to a quasi-suicidal sensibility that has led him to follow 'the sinful, hasty, satanic and *easy* path of the Destruction of myself' (Mallarmé's emphasis). Rather than accede by natural stages to a plateau of sustainable inner detachment and spiritual strength he is conscious instead of the total physical exhaustion that follows upon prolonged poetic endeavour: 'after a few days of mental and spiritual tension spent in my apartment I become frozen, an image reflected in the diamond of this mirror before me – to the point where it is like a death agony: and then when I want to revive myself in earthly sunshine, the sun melts me – it reveals to me the profound disaggregation of my physical being, and I become aware of my complete exhaustion.' Above all, he tells Lefébure, 'I must, by taking meticulous care in the way I live, avoid total meltdown – which is certain to begin with my chest' (*Corr.*, I. 247).

The two 'chasms' that Mallarmé had mentioned to Cazalis in April 1866 with relative equanimity – 'Nothingness' and his chest – were now yawning more alarmingly. The cold, damp climate of Besançon was particularly bad for his lungs, and he yearned for the south. Summer holidays spent on a farm in the mountains near Besançon helped somewhat, but Mallarmé was delighted when his application to be transferred to Avignon was accepted. The family moved there on 12 October and soon found a pretty terraced house: the fig tree and oleander bushes growing in the front garden bore testimony to its welcome climate, as did the vine that trailed from its facade. But the Mistral wind had not gone away, and in December he fell very seriously ill with pleuro-pneumonia. His grandmother, fearing for his life, came all the way from Versailles to help Marie look after him. Thereafter the Avignon climate did more good than ill, and in late August and early September 1868 a long summer holiday spent on the Mediterranean coast would bring further improvement. 'Sometimes', he had told Lefébure in May 1867, 'I just want to be a beggar in Africa!' (*Corr.*, I. 247).

But Mallarmé's chest was not the only source of pain. Reading and writing poetry involved 'sensations', and his 'terrifying year' of poetic adventure had itself been one of physical suffering. In the May 1867 letter he tells Cazalis of the 'horrible sensibility' that has brought him these new discoveries, and he redeploys the terms in his letter to Lefébure a fortnight later. In September 1867 (*Corr.*, I. 259) he elaborates on this to Villiers: 'By virtue of a deep sensibility I came to see the intimate correlation between Poetry and the Universe, and, in order for this correlation to be pure, conceived the plan of extracting Poetry from the realm of Dream and Chance and aligning it with the conception of the Universe.' But this conception has not been the result of exclusively mental activity: 'you will be terrified to learn that I have arrived at the Idea of the Universe by sensation alone (and that, for example, in order to retain an indelible notion of pure Nothingness, I had to impose on my brain the sensation of an absolute void).'

The two chasms thus combined into a third, which threatened to engulf him: nervous exhaustion. From mid-1867 for a period of approximately three years Mallarmé suffered a prolonged nervous illness punctuated by periods of apparent remission. In his correspondence later that year he dates the origins of the condition back to the previous winter: 'I have spent the most miserable year of my life', he tells Aubanel in October, 'undermined by an illness that I simply don't understand' (*Corr.*, I. 263). But by the following spring he has come to recognize Easter 1866 as the key moment. On 3 May he informs Lefébure:

> I am in a state of crisis that cannot continue, and that is my one consolation! Either I'll get worse or I'll get better . . . Clearly I'm on my way back down from the absolute . . . but my two-year-long relationship with it (do you remember? since we were in Cannes together?) will leave a mark on me that I firmly intend to consecrate. I'm on my way back down into my self, which I abandoned two years ago: and, after all, poems that are even just tinged with the absolute are already beautiful, and there are so few of them – not to mention the fact that reading them in the future will bring back the poet I dreamt of being . . . (*Corr.*, I. 273)

But consolation was denied him as the crisis continued. By the following January he has come to believe that he must accept the condition as permanent. His doctor now told him not to write at all, even a letter, and from February 1869 his correspondence is effected by Marie under dictation. Through her he continues to update Cazalis: 'my thinking process, for so long occupied and distended by the fullness of the Universe, was losing its normal function: I became conscious that the mere act of writing was causing some very worrying symptoms, and hysteria was beginning to disrupt my spoken use of language' (*Corr.*, I. 299). He remains determined to fight on – 'for you, my dear friends, to whom I owe a Book' (*Corr.*, I. 301) – but insomnia is a new enemy (and remained so throughout the rest of his life). In May he was too ill even to attend his grandmother's funeral in Versailles. Summer holidays spent with Marie and Vève at Lecques on the Mediterranean coast brought improvement, as they had the year before, but in December he tells Renaud of the illness in his chest being once more exacerbated by the winter climate and informs Cazalis of his 'cataleptic absence', which has taken hold once more 'despite my ruses' (*Corr.*, I. 315).

Relief came at last in January 1870 when he was granted six months' sick leave, on half pay (1,000 francs p.a.). He would supplement this with income (perhaps 500 francs) from the public English lessons that the Mayor had permitted him to give in one of his public rooms for the benefit of the young people of Avignon. His wife had also recently purchased a state franchise on a tobacconist's in Arles (perhaps with a legacy?), and this was bringing in 400 francs p.a. And he would study. For one of his 'ruses' was to fight like with like: to occupy his mind homeo-pathically with new mental horizons that would hold the old obsessions at bay. In short, he would 'take advantage of this leave to repair my life a little, my health and my career also' (*Corr.*, I. 317). Accordingly he resurrected his former plan to write a doctorate, for which he would first have to study for the Licence: 'suddenly I face the curious and interesting prospect of a year's Latin and Greek' (*Corr.*, I. 314). He has chosen linguistics, he tells Lefébure on 20 March, in the hope that such study may have a beneficial influence on 'the whole apparatus of language which seems to be the principal target of my nervous illness' (*Corr.*, I. 318). With what little German he possesses he plans soon to tackle a comparative grammar on the Indo-European languages (including especially Sanskrit), and this by way of preparing to be awarded the Licence in two years' time. Thereafter he will spend three years on a doctorate. And, of course, he has the topic for his thesis already: 'since I have been stupid enough to aim straight for my Idea and to deny myself the progressive seduction of its mirages.'

And his Great Work? 'Alongside all that', he continues, 'the work of my heart and solitude is very slowly taking shape, and I can glimpse its structure: in truth the other, parallel labour is simply its scientific foundation.' From this it is clear that the 'Great Work' – 'the Book' that he owed his friends – was intended to embody fundamental correlations between language and the 'Universe', and that Mallarmé was intent on studying the history of languages in order to pursue further the ideas to which Lefébure had introduced him regarding the role of language in the creation of myth and the origins of religion. Indeed in March Lefébure had congratulated Mallarmé on his plans, not only because they would constitute a healthy antidote to undue self-preoccupation but also because 'linguistics . . . is the science of the future': 'today, with historical knowledge stretching further and further back into the past, the origins of man can be glimpsed through the various strata in which languages have left the footprints of human thinking superimposed upon the early traces of the primitive mind' (*Corr.*, I. 319–20, n. 1). Language was itself a kind of fossil record. Lefébure is thinking here especially of the pioneering work of the German philologist Franz Bopp, who with his compatriot Jacob Grimm and the Danish scholar Rasmus Rask had revolutionized the study of historical linguistics.

It is clear also that this link between Mallarmé's poetic project and his ambitions for an academic study of language date back at least to May 1868. At this point in his prolonged crisis he had not 'written an alexandrine for two years' (*oc*, I. 729), but now he began writing poetry again, and draft versions of two sonnets have survived from this period. This was the moment at which he described himself to Lefébure as being on his way ' back down from the absolute' and 'back down into my self ', and the two poems bear distinct autobiographical traces of his current anguish. They also set a new trend, for from this point on Mallarmé's verse output is almost entirely in sonnet form. Given his determination to 'extract Poetry from the realm of Dream and Chance', Mallarmé found the fixed form of the sonnet more satisfactory than the various binary structures that he had devised earlier in the decade.

The first of these sonnets, in octosyllabic metre, was sent on 2 July to Bonaparte Wyse, a wealthy Irishman descended on his mother's side from Napoleon's younger brother Lucien. A poet also, Wyse was a fervent admirer and patron of the Félibres, through whom Mallarmé had met him, and he had himself published poems in Occitan. The sonnet reads:

De l'orient passé des Temps
Nulle étoffe jadis venue
Ne vaut la chevelure nue
Que loin des bijoux tu détends.

Moi qui vis parmi les tentures
Pour ne pas voir le Néant seul,
Mes yeux, las de ces sépultures,
Aimeraient ce divin linceul.

Mais tandis que les rideaux vagues
Cachent des ténèbres les vagues
Mortes, hélas! ces beaux cheveux

Lumineux en l'esprit font naître
D'atroces étincelles d'Être,
Mon horreur et mes désaveux.

From the old orient of days gone by / no fabric previously come / can match the naked hair / that, far from jewels, you unpin and let fall. / As to me who lives among draperies / in order not to see the Nothingness alone, / my eyes, tired of these graves and burials, / would love [to wrap itself in] this divine shroud.

/ But while the vague curtains / conceal the dead waves [also, the shadowy dead women] of the darkness, alas! this beautiful hair, / luminous in the mind, gives birth / to cruel sparks of Being, / my horror and my disavowals [also, spawns / from out of cruel sparks of Being / my horror and my disavowals.

In essence the poet is describing the temptation presented by his beloved's hair as a source of solace in the world of objects. If we imagine a poet who had specifically sought to fashion a new kind of poetry by undermining the conventional referential function of language, then here in the octave of this sonnet we see him temporarily wanting to shut his eyes to the 'Nothingness' which this abolition of reference entails. Having 'died' to the world of objects (hence his need of a shroud), his eyes are weary of the sepulchral absences of the void: instead he would rather bury his perception in the beauty of this golden hair – a beauty that is natural ('far from jewels') and surpassing that of any man-made fabric known to history. The sestet, however, inverts the sequence of the octave: the first tercet tells how the shadowy curtains of a non-mimetic linguistic world in fact conceal the 'death' of the waves (of real hair), while the second tercet reveals how the very luminosity of the hair sharpens his mental horror (as a poet) at the world of objects, a world he has disavowed. The values of light and dark are exchanged, so that the conventional illumination of mimetic imagery is replaced by the welcome obscurity of non-representational poetry. The golden gleam of hair and the glitter of jewels have turned into the sparks of some cruel, excruciating torture – perhaps the anguished awareness of the inevitable gap between language and material reality. At the same time the potentially funereal 'draperies' have become 'the vague curtains', with their connotations of refuge and domestic comfort.

But the principal strategy of the poem is to transmute the gold of the hair into a motif that is incorporated into the unrivalled linguistic fabric of the text itself. The French word for gold – 'or' – rises overtly in the first line, like the golden sun itself, in the 'orient' but remains implicit in the enfolded, curtained darkness of non-referential language ('les vagues / M*or*tes'); then it is obfuscated, reversed, in 'at*ro*ces' (the golden sparks of the hair provide the wrong kind of gold) before appearing at the end in 'h*or*reur' in symmetrical counterpoint to the 'De l'or' with which the poem homophonically began. This linguistic fabric is intricately patterned in many other ways, notably in its almost exclusively rich rhymes, and its threads combine in a text(ure) that is at once tantalizingly insubstantial and yet rich with suggestion and interconnection. The beauty of the hair has been replaced by the luminosity of a sonnet which is as bereft of obvious referents in the world as the hair itself is unadorned and yet which, among the tresses of its rhymes, sparkles with the jewels of a quasi-stellar mystery. In the context the last word – 'désaveux' – begins to sound like 'dés-aveux', dice-avowals: as though poetry were much less the autobiography of one man's identifiable anguish than a series of utterly contingent statements governed by the 'vague' and mysterious logic of language itself.

Mallarmé continued to work on this poem – another early manuscript version, provisionally entitled 'Alternative' has also survived – but it was not published in its definitive and even more complex form until 1885, as 'Quelle soie aux baumes de temps . . .' (What silk imbued with the balms of time . . .). And there is good reason to suppose that several of the sonnets eventually published in the 1887 *Poésies* may have first come into being during this 'descent from the Absolute'.

The other poem of which a draft version survives from this period – the sonnet in alexandrines entitled 'Sonnet allégorique de lui-même' (Sonnet allegorical of itself) – was sent by Mallarmé to Cazalis on 18 July 1868. It also demonstrates clearly that some kind of correlation between poetry and the universe, and in particular between the 'solar drama' and a linguistic play with

Ses purs ongles très haut dédiant leur onyx,
L'Angoisse ce minuit, soutient, lampadophore
Maint rêve vespéral brûlé par le Phénix
Que ne recueille pas de cinéraire amphore

Sur les crédences, au salon vide : nul ptyx,
Aboli bibelot d'inanité sonore,
(Car le Maître est allé puiser des pleurs au Styx
Avec ce seul objet dont le Néant s'honore.)

Mais proche la croisée au nord vacante, un or
Agonise selon peut-être le décor
Des licornes ruant du feu contre une nixe,

Elle, défunte nue en le miroir encor
Que dans l'oubli fermé par le cadre se fixe
De scintillations sitôt le septuor.

'Ses purs ongles . . .', the revised version of the 'Sonnet allégorique de lui-même',
was first published in *Poésies* (1887), which reproduced Mallarmé's manuscript
copies by photolithography.

the word 'or', was uppermost in the poet's mind at the time. The
publisher Lemerre was planning a volume of sonnets, each to be
accompanied by a separately commissioned etching, and Cazalis –
perhaps to take his friend's mind off his troubles – had pressed him
to submit something. With only a week's notice, in stifling heat, and
still during term-time, Mallarmé felt harrassed, but he could see the
value of the opportunity.

This poem later became the so-called 'Sonnet en yx', beginning
'Ses purs ongles, très haut dédiant leurs onyx . . .' (Its pure nails

very high dedicating their onyx . . .), and was first published in 1887. It is perhaps Mallarmé's most famous sonnet. In its first version it constitutes a key moment in the evolution of his poetic art, and indeed approximates closely to that 'consecration' of his 'two-year-long relationship with the absolute' that he had mentioned to Lefébure in the letter of 3 May – especially as in this letter Mallarmé mentions a sonnet he has in mind and asks his friend about the meaning of the word 'ptyx', which he requires as a fourth rhyme on 'ix'. The poem reads, in this early version:

> *La Nuit approbatrice allume les onyx*
> *De ses ongles au pur Crime, lampadophore,*
> *Du Soir aboli par le vespéral Phœnix*
> *De qui la cendre n'a de cinéraire amphore*
>
> *Sur des consoles, en le noir Salon: nul ptyx,*
> *Insolite vaisseau d'inanité sonore,*
> *Car le Maître est allé puiser de l'eau du Styx*
> *Avec tous ses objets dont le Rêve s'honore.*
>
> *Et selon la croisée au Nord vacante, un or*
> *Néfaste incite pour son beau cadre une rixe*
> *Faite d'un dieu que croit emporter une nixe*
>
> *En l'obscurcissement de la glace, décor*
> *De l'absence, sinon que sur la glace encor*
> *De scintillations le septuor se fixe.*

The approving Night lights the onyx / of its nails on the pure Crime, torchbearer, / of the Evening abolished by the vesperal Phoenix / the ash of which has no cinerary amphora / on console tables, in the black drawing-room: no ptyx, / unusual vessel of sonorous inanity, / for the Master has gone

to draw water from the Styx / with all these objects with which
(the) Dream honours itself. / And following the casement open
wide to the North, a gold [*sic*], / ill-fated, incites as a fine frame
for itself a scuffle / created by a god whom a nixie believes
herself to be carrying off / in the darkening of the mirror,
a décor / of absence, except that on the mirror still / the septet
of scintillas fixes itself.

Mallarmé realized that the poem might be insufficiently mimetic
for Lemerre's purpose and sought to persuade Cazalis, his intermediary, that it could nevertheless accompany an etching that
depicted the following scene (observed from outside):

an open window at night-time, with both shutters fastened
back against the wall; a room with no one inside, despite
the appearance of peaceful habitation suggested by the open
shutters, and on a night made of absence and interrogation,
without furniture, except the plausible outline of dimly perceived console tables, and a mirror hanging in the background,
its frame bellicose and writhing in a death agony, and with its
unfathomable stellar reflection of the Great Bear, which alone
connects this forsaken lodging-place with the sky. (*Corr.*, I. 279)

But at the heart of the poem – 'a nothing-sonnet reflecting itself
in all sorts of ways', as Mallarmé described it (Corr, I. 279) – is a
correlation between the seven stars of a constellation and the form
of the Petrarchan sonnet. Reflected in a mirror these seven stars
become the fourteen lines of a sonnet, and the double quatrains
and double tercets of the poem may suggest a duplication of the
four-star square of the Great Bear (or Big Dipper) with its 'tail' of
three stars. Where the octave describes an absence, as though the
disappearance of the sun has left only darkness and the void, the
sestet suggests the presence of some salvaged light – in the gleam,

perhaps, of a gilded mirror-frame and in the stars reflected within the mirror itself. The sonnet is allegorical of itself also because the rhyme on 'or' that 'gleams' in the octave and suggests that light is sound ('phore'/ 'sonore') is itself 'saved' in the rhyme-frame of the tercets ('un or', 'décor', 'encor'). By choosing words for their sound – the 'crime of rhyme' – the sonnet creates its own vessel, in the apparent absence of a controlling poet-master who has gone to draw the means of expressing nothingness out of the very waters of the Styx. For 'ptyx' – a hapax legomenon unattested in French and attested in Ancient Greek only in the dative plural (meaning 'folds') – has been 'born' of the need for a rich rhyme with 'Styx' (i.e. sharing at least its last three phonetic elements); and this non-existent word, like this 'nothing-sonnet', comes thereby to symbolize the plenitude and 'multiplication' that is to be won from the 'inanity' (etymologically, blankness) of apparently meaningless sound.

Mallarmé claimed in his letter to Cazalis to have 'extracted' this poem 'from a projected study of *the Spoken Word* [*la Parole*]', and it would seem therefore that an important part of Mallarmé's thinking about the 'scientific foundation' for his Great Work at this stage was focused on the way in which language can generate novel scenarios. Here the simple decision to create a poem with end-rhymes in 'ix(e)' and 'or(e)' has produced its own storyline, a new 'myth' that figures the old, old story of the solar passage. Central to rhyme and to this process of creation is the homophonic power of language, the whispers of like-sounding words and syllables that produce the *Idée*. This may explain why in some fragmentary hand-written notes that have also survived from this period (*oc*, I. 503–12) we can see that the topic of 'conversation' is central. For it is in the spoken use of language (as implied earlier by the poet's insistence that *L'Après-midi d'un faune* demanded the theatre as a context for its performance) that its 'rhyming' ambiguities are most manifest. Manuscript and print make the meanings of words seem much more self-evident than they really are; whereas 'words have several meanings, otherwise we would always understand each other perfectly'. The spoken word, he argues, creates 'analogies between things by creating analogies between sounds', whereas writing records 'the gestures of the Idea as it manifests itself via the spoken word [by] offering to [these gestures] their own reflection, in such a way as to complete them in the present (in the process of reading), and to conserve them in the future as annals of the successive stages of linguistic activity and of its filiation: and to show the relations between them.'

At the heart of these notes lies a strong distinction between 'Verbe' (the Word, the Verbum) and 'langage', which Saussure would formulate a few decades later as the difference between 'langue' and 'parole' (respectively, language as system and language as practice). There is also concomitant emphasis on the act of linguistic utterance as a shifting, transient attempt to 'abstract' the 'notion' from a material object or phenomenon. Conversation is the key 'linguistic site' where through (at least) two interlocutors parallel processes of such 'abstraction' enter into dialogue and thereby put the possibility of sharing 'knowledge' to the test. Only by knowing what language does and how it operates can we know what we know.

Mallarmé was particularly fascinated by the fact that linguistics is the one intellectual discipline in which the subject and medium of analysis are the same, and the phrase 'language reflecting itself' stands out amidst his somewhat cryptic notes as an indication of the direction in which both his poetic practice and his academic study of language were taking him. Since all 'science' is couched in language, then perhaps the study of language will reveal to us the true nature – indeed perhaps the 'fictive' nature – of human knowledge. And perhaps poetry could be the most penetrating means of investigating 'la Science du langage': literally, 'the science of language' but also, more interestingly, 'what language knows about itself '. For all linguistic constructs are 'fictions' (a key term in these notes), just as poetry and *poésies* are 'fashionings' and 'fabrications'. The supplementary thesis, in Latin, that a doctoral student was then required to submit in addition to the principal thesis, would – Mallarmé here envisages – be entitled 'De divinitate'. As Müller was arguing, mythological deities are the products of language, a projection into a 'beyond' of symbols that figure and palliate our anguished human condition. And to 'divine' (in French, *deviner*) is to know or speak of hidden things, like a soothsayer, or like a poet intimating knowledge of a silent mystery.

In the event Mallarmé's intellectual and literary ambitions in these areas would find alternative outlets during the following decade. But for the moment his poetic work during the late 1860s – the two sonnets we have and others that may have been begun at this period – provided a means of exploring and exemplifying these issues. The unfinished and unpublished prose tale entitled *Igitur* provides a further, tantalizing glimpse of his thoughts at this time. In July 1869 he tells Cazalis that he is at work: 'for in fact otherwise [my] illness gets worse and to no purpose. If I can finally extract from it a beautiful prose tale, then you shall have it' (*Corr.*, I. 305). In November he promises him for the following summer 'a prose tale by which I intend to put paid to the old monster of Impotence – which is its subject indeed – so that I can cloister myself in my great labour, which I've already been studying afresh. If I can bring it off (the tale), I am cured: *similia similibus*' (*Corr.*, I. 313). Whether or not he ever sent Cazalis a copy, this attempted homeopathic cure to his ills seems to have worked to the extent that he was able to read from a version of this tale to other friends the following August. Villiers de l'Isle-Adam and Catulle Mendès, with his wife Judith Gautier, had been visiting Wagner at his home in Tribschen on Lake Lucerne (where the latter lived from 1866 to 1872), but were now returning home to France following the outbreak of the Franco-Prussian war. They stopped off at Avignon to see Mallarmé, who treated them to a performance that left them – as Mendès recalled several decades later – decidedly nonplussed.

Owing not only to the incomplete nature of the surviving text but also to the strangeness and density of the writing, it is difficult to infer unambiguous import from *Igitur*, but the outlines of the plot suggest a Gothic allegory of the ordeal that its author had recently undergone. Moreover the text has a decidedly theatrical complexion: 'this tale is addressed to the Intelligence of the reader[,] which stages its various elements itself'. The setting for this form of mental theatre is a room in a castle, at midnight. In this claustrophobic chamber, hung with heavy draperies, are a mirror, a clock, and a table upon which stand a book and a candle – and, possibly, a glass phial. The sole protagonist, Igitur (from the Latin, meaning 'thus'), is the last descendant of an ancient race and finds himself called upon by a prediction contained within the book to fulfil an an age-old, dynastic duty and to perform an act that is considered to abolish chance. Taking the book and candle with him he leaves the room and descends into a crypt containing the tombs of his ancestors. There, though conscious of the futility of his act (which will not abolish chance), he complies with his destiny and accomplishes the act: either by drinking from the phial (presumably in a form of suicide) or by throwing (or possibly just shaking) two dice. Thereupon he closes the book, blows out the candle, and lies down (presumably to die) upon the ashes of his ancestors.

Vestiges of this suggestive plot were later radically reworked to form the basis of Mallarmé's most innovative poem, *Un coup de Dés jamais n'abolira le Hasard* (A Throw of the Dice Never Will Abolish Chance), first published in 1897, but here it seems to represent the fate of the writer, paralysed (or rendered 'impotent') by an intuitive awareness of the 'Absolute' and yet obliged to submit to some pointless act that will never overcome the contingency of a godless universe. At one level this is an allegory about the mirage of necessity that may surround the act of suicide as a willed embrace of contingent mortality; at another it is the story of a writer who knows that any linguistic act, however concerted, is simply a game of chance played with potentialities of language that will always exceed his knowing and his control. In these readings 'Igitur' is the ironic name for a doomed victim of the aleatory. But the nature of the writing in *Igitur* gives the lie to this reading, for it abounds in wordplay and all manner of suggestive linguistic patterning. Here, as in the 'Sonnet allégorique de lui-même', the fact that the two words 'son or' (his/her/its gold; sound-gold) can be 'refined' from the very word 'sonorité' (*oc*, I. 483) is emblematic of the quasi-alchemical power of poetic language to transform the contingent into seeming necessity.

Part of the manuscript of *Igitur* contains speculative linguistic 'doodlings' that show the writer's hand more clearly. We see him playing, for example, with the word *heure* (hour) and its homophone *heurt* (jolt) – it is the midnight hour that 'jolts' Igitur into action. The word produces the story. Most telling of all is the sequence 'plus se plu me plume' (*oc*, I. 866). A *plume* (a feather, and the writer's pen) is (homophonically) 'plus me' – meaning indirectly (since grammatically one would need the personal pronoun *moi* not the reflexive pronoun *me*) 'no longer me' but also 'more me'. The act of writing is itself a form of suicide: a farewell to the contingencies of the individual writer's subjectivity but simultaneously a poetically empowering accession to a timeless, 'dynastic' role as the agent of language: an 'instrument' through which the 'universe' speaks (as he had put it the previous year). It is this kind of linguistic play that explains in part the intended subtitle of *Igitur*: *La Folie d'Elbehnon*. 'Folie' (folly, madness) is anagrammatically related to the *fiole* (phial) that is the means of Igitur's fulfilment of his destiny: a crazy scrambling of letters. As to Elbehnon, no one has yet been able to explain satisfactorily to whom or what 'Elbehnon' might be a reference. Perhaps it recalls the 'juice of cursed hebenon in a vial' from which Hamlet's father died (*Hamlet*, I, v). Or perhaps it is some mythical place, to be found along the way that madness lies. Like a chasm.

4

Tombs

Just as Mallarmé was emerging from the chasm of his nervous illness in the spring and early summer of 1870, his wife Marie fell seriously ill with a liver complaint. Vève, now five, had become something of a handful and, even though her father was on leave, arrangements were made to have her looked after by a local boarding-school during the afternoons. Mallarmé himself was in the grip of 'a most tyrannical labour' (*Corr.*, v. 204). By the end of May Marie was still suffering badly 'almost day and night' (*Corr.*, i. 326), and in late July, as the school year began to draw to a close, Mallarmé wrote to Mistral requesting him to use a particularly well-placed friend at the Ministry of Education to secure him a further period of leave: 'I am not wholly recovered and in no state to resume teaching' (*Corr.* i. 330). Furthermore, he argued, 'the Lycée was partly the cause of my nervous illness'.

Mallarmé was more convinced than ever that he really could not return to teaching, and he began to dream of some future career based in Paris. However, following the outbreak of the Franco-Prussian War on 19 July 1870 and the disastrous French defeat at Sedan on 2 September, Paris itself was now under siege, and so for the moment sabbatical leave in Avignon was much the safer bet. In November he received belated word (delayed by the war) granting an extension of his leave for the whole academic year.

On 18 January 1871 the union of the German empire was proclaimed at Versailles, and Wilhelm i of Prussia crowned there as its first Kaiser. On the following day one last, doomed, attempt was made to break the siege, by a French assault launched at Buzenval not far from Versailles, and it was here that Mallarmé's friend Henri Régnault met his death. His body was never identified. The night before the battle the painter had been at a party with friends (Villiers, Mendès, and others) at the Versailles home of Augusta Holmès, a gifted musician, composer and poet of Anglo-Irish extraction, god-daughter of the famous writer Alfred de Vigny and thought by many, because of their physical resemblance, to be his daughter. She was now Mendès' mistress (and would eventually have four children by him). At midnight, as the party was coming to an end, Régnault sang a song written to the music of Saint-Saëns by their mutual friend, Armand Renaud. Its lyrics included the lines: 'Here by this white tomb / We mingle our tears' (*Corr.*, I. 337, n. 1). His friends would have several occasions to quote them over the coming decade.

Mallarmé and Cazalis shared their common grief by letter, both of them shattered by this first and unexpected 'void' in their circle of friends and bitterly angry at the stupid waste of such a talent. For Mallarmé in particular the loss was especially poignant since in the very same letter he also informs Cazalis of a further 'misfortune': Marie is expecting their second child. The life-cycle continues. Vêve, of course, is delighted, but her parents deeply apprehensive. Both of them have been seriously ill: will they be able to cope? Marie's pregnancy proved arduous, particularly as she neared her term during a very hot summer; and for his own part Mallarmé remained acutely wary of a recurrence of his illness. He had to 'manage' it, to outwit it by 'regular ruse' and stratagem (*Corr.*, I. 339–40, 344). Never-theless his 'vocation' (*Corr.*, I. 342) was now clear. Having abandoned further thought of academic study, he announces to Cazalis in March that 'I am a writer again, pure and simple'. Moreover:

> My work is no longer a myth. (One volume of Prose Tales, dreamt of. One volume of Poetry, glimpsed and murmured.

One volume of Criticism, or what we used to call the Universe, considered from a strictly *literary* point of view.) In sum, enough to fill my mornings for the next twenty years. [Mallarmé's emphasis]

Mallarmé was now also working on a play, in prose: a 'Drama and a Vaudeville' that would 'discredit Art and Science in the eyes of an attentive Public for a number of years to come' (*Corr.*, I. 352). Presumably he believed that his new insights regarding the relationship between language and knowledge would make contemporary thinking about 'Art and Science' seem outmoded and wrong. He hoped to submit the play for production that coming autumn, but no further trace of this project has been found. The Great Work, however, lived on: 'these critical hours [as his health recovers in April 1871 following a difficult winter] allow me to glimpse flashes of what was my dream for four years, a dream so often endangered. But I still have it in my grasp, more or less' (*Corr.*, I. 351).

But this is more or less the last we hear of the Great Work – in these terms at least – for the next fourteen years. During this period Mallarmé would hold fast to his determination to publish only when the whole edifice was complete. Like Igitur he was going underground – to 'sculpt his own tomb', as he later put it (*oc*, II. 700). Or, as he also wrote (*oc*, II. 217), he was entering a tunnel, like the one that trains were then obliged to traverse under the Place de l'Europe before entering the 'glass palace' of the Gare St Lazare: a dark, lonely journey through the chasm of nothingness towards the dazzling light of a new poetic perfection.

Following the end of the siege of Paris, and later the brutal suppression of the Paris Commune at the end of May, it was possible to envisage a return to the capital. Henri Régnault's fiancée, Geneviève Bréton, had heard of Mallarmé's wish, and sought to honour her fiancé's memory and his friendship with the poet by using her influence as a member of the wealthy family that controlled the major publishing company Hachette. Moreover the Minister of Education, Jules Simon, was a friend. But Mallarmé himself was envisaging some kind of part-time employment that would leave him sufficient leisure for his own creative writing and perhaps also – to supplement his income – for some journalism. Des Essarts warned him against it as a form of enslavement worse even than teaching, but Villiers had mentioned the possibility of writing a weekly article for *L'Illustration* (Paris's answer to the *Illustrated London News*), which would bring in 1,000 francs a year. Or perhaps he could be the foreign correspondent of a London newspaper? Then there was the possibility of translation work, and he had ideas, too, for a number of teaching manuals and an anthology of recent English poetry. If necessary, he would undertake private tuition. A post as librarian would be ideal, like Coppée's at the Senate, or the one Lefébure also had his eye on.

Responding to invitations from Anna Mallarmé in Sens and from Catulle Mendès in Paris, the Mallarmés left Avignon at the end of May 1871: Mallarmé, in the company of Des Essarts (now posted to Nîmes), had paid a special farewell visit to Mistral. Marie was to stay with Anna and her family in Sens and have her baby there. Stéphane meanwhile would share Mendès's large modern house at Neuilly, on the western fringe of the city, and seek work. The Mallarmé's second child was born on 16 July. The baby had fair hair and blue eyes, like his mother, and was to be called Anatole, like Mallarmé's priestly cousin, Anatole Rain, whom they had got to know in Besançon and who would be godfather. Mallarmé, detained in Paris at the time of the birth, could spare little time (or money) to visit, and in August he soon departed for London, where he hoped to cover the International Exhibition for four Paris newspapers. It was a chance to earn some money and renew old friendships: with Bonaparte Wyse, who had invited him, and also with the Yapp family, whom he had first encountered at that memorable picnic in Fontainebleau and who were back in London for the summer. Ettie Yapp herself was now a journalist like her father, co-writing articles about Paris with her two sisters (under a single pseudonym) for *The Queen*, the principal women's magazine of the day.

The International Exhibition of 1871, held in South Kensington, was envisaged as a further sequel (following that of 1862) to the extraordinary 1851 Great Exhibition of the Works of Industry of All Nations, with its celebrated 'Crystal Palace' in Hyde Park (later re-sited at Sydenham in south London). The Great Exhibition had attracted some six million visitors from home and abroad (equivalent to a third of the then population of Great Britain itself), and famously drawn the ire of Karl Marx for its promotion of fetishistic consumerism. Its 1871 successor (like those held annually for the next three years) represented something like an 'Ideal Homes' exhibition, and the poet who had once contemplated the twin chasms of Nothingness and his chest was now to be seen each morning between the hours of eight and ten, notepad and pencil in hand, surveying the latest masterpieces of 'industrial art': furniture of all kinds, clocks and lamps in bronze or porcelain, candelabras and statuettes, etc., etc. But this was also the poet who had bought his wife a clock in Dresden china and blown an inheritance on Venetian mirrors and Louis Quatorze chairs, a man who felt a deep fascination for the silent histories of antique objects. Here before him, like newly written poems, were the antiques of the future, carefully wrought artefacts that unwittingly and sometimes wittingly embodied the solar drama in their golden representations of time and light. Like Poe, Mallarmé had his own 'philosophy of furniture'.

That the solar drama was rarely far from Mallarmé's mind may be seen at this time also in his efforts to secure from Longmans the translation rights to *A Manual of Mythology in the Form of Question and Answer* published in 1867 by the Reverend George William

Cox. Cox, a firm believer in the recent theories of Max Müller, had more recently published his comprehensive, popularizing study *The Mythology of the Aryan Nations* (2 vols, 1870), but Mallarmé could see the advantages of the earlier work as a textbook for French schools. His translation-cum-adaptation would appear eventually in 1880 under the title *Les Dieux antiques* (The Gods of Antiquity), and subtitled 'A New Mythology'. For Mallarmé the antique deities by which we project our human predicament onto the skies above were no less fascinating than the word or the antique chair.

In the event only one newspaper (*Le National*) took up Mallarmé's offer of copy on the International Exhibition, and so only three articles have survived from this visit, each signed 'L. S. Price' – a double pun on £.s.d. (pre-decimal pounds, shillings and pence) and the French 'l'esprit' (the French for 'price' being 'prix'). Thus the material world of furniture, clocks, lamps, jewellery, ceramics, upholstery and rugs has been interpreted by a mind that knows the symbolic as well as monetary worth of objects. In these articles Mallarmé is particularly attuned to the 'fusion of art and industry' (*oc*, ii. 366) manifest in the complementary phenomena of high art being applied to 'products required by our immediate needs' and of the techniques of high art themselves being multiplied and made available to an ever-growing number of people by the possibility of mass production. The utilitarian was being transformed by art while art itself was being democratized. This chimed with the poet's growing conviction that poetry not only brings 'beautiful' pattern to the tools of quotidian utterance but also has the capacity to answer the spiritual needs of a potentially universal populace. A lamp can be the emblem of the solar drama: a crystal inkwell can suggest the stellar brilliance to be penned from the darkness of the night.

Hence the symbolic furniture of so many of Mallarmé's poems begun or revised as part of his 'sculpting of the tomb' during the late 1860s and the 1870s. Take, for example, the console table that figures at the end of 'Tout Orgueil fume-t-il du soir . . .', with its writhing, S-shaped legs and the gilt that catches a gleam of the dying sun with which to 'console' our anguish, just as the tomb-like sonnet itself preserves the 'or' [gold] from the '*or*gueil [pride]' of a proud sun brought low. Witness also the 'lampadophore' (a torch-bearing relay runner in ancient games, or a candelabra representing one) that entered into the later revision of the 'Sonnet en yx' as a word that helps to relay the syllable 'or' from one end of this poem to the other.

Following his visits to the Exhibition Mallarmé travelled down to see Bonaparte Wyse at his home in Bradford-on-Avon in Wiltshire. Through him he met the English poet John Payne, who had recently published his collection of sonnets entitled *Intaglios* and was soon to become a celebrated translator (notably of *The Thousand and One Nights*). The two poets became firm friends and active correspondents. For the moment Payne urged Mallarmé to read the poems of Algernon Swinburne. Later he would provide key entrées into the literary and artistic world of London.

On his return to Paris Mallarmé realized that his financial situation was becoming desperate. The war and the events of the Commune had badly disrupted the administration of the country: he was owed arrears on his salary, and Marie's nest-egg income from the tobacconist's in Arles was also overdue. The offer of a job teaching French on the British training ship HMS *Trafalgar* looked almost attractive. In mid-September Mallarmé learnt by letter from Marie, who had wished to spare him, that Anatole had been very seriously ill and on the point of death. A renewed crisis at the end of the month brought Mallarmé to his son's cradle immediately, and once more everyone feared the worst. But again the baby survived.

His friends continued to rally round in the hope of finding him a job, and in the end Geneviève Bréton's influence at the Ministry of Education paid off. At first the authorities offered to reappoint him to his previous post at Avignon, but for Mallarmé there was no going back. Instead, by great good fortune, some newly created posts in Modern Languages had become available in Paris (just as he had once promised his grandfather they would!), and he was appointed on 25 October to a position at the Lycée Condorcet at a salary of 270 francs a month. Unfortunately the appointment also brought additional teaching duties at the Lycée Saint-Louis, which would involve almost daily journeys across Paris to the top of the Boulevard Saint-Michel. A month later he and his family moved into a four-room apartment on the fourth floor at 29 rue de Moscou, not far from the Lycée Condorcet on the rue du Havre and that other 'crystal palace', the Gare Saint-Lazare.

The return to teaching spurred Mallarmé's efforts to find ways of not teaching. The experience of writing on the International Exhibition, for example, seems to have inspired the idea, first mentioned to Heredia in April 1872, of founding a new monthly magazine entitled *L'Art Décoratif*. He had mock-ups of the cover produced and tried to raise subscriptions among his friends, but nothing further came of it. Somehow he managed another visit to London in July, to report on that year's International Exhibition. One article in *L'Illustration* alone was published (though two further draft articles survive), and in it the visitor marvels at the recently opened Royal Albert Hall (its exterior if not its interior) and pokes fun at the municipal orderliness of the surrounding gardens. Where is the delightful informality of the *jardin anglais* that had once offered French royalty merciful relief from the symmetries of the classical parterre?

For all his extra-curricular activities Mallarmé's teaching was effective, and he received favourable reports towards the end of his first school year in Paris from both his headmaster and the inspector. But the exhausting demands (and commuting) imposed on him by his role at the Lycée Saint-Louis were endangering the newly won equilibrium of his nerves, and he felt obliged to ask to be relieved of them – and therefore of half his salary. Fortunately an old friend from the Tournon days, Charles Seignobos, now a député for the Ardèche, added his support to the efforts of Geneviève Bréton and her father: Mallarmé was promoted at the Lycée Condorcet and his salary restored to its former level of approximately 3,300 francs per annum. Further pressure would secure an additional 500 francs the following January.

Now aged 28 and more or less securely settled in Paris, Mallarmé was able to revel fully in the company of all the poets he had met over recent years – Cazalis, Mendès and Villiers, of course, but also Leconte de Lisle, Banville, Heredia, Glatigny, Dierx, Coppée, Charles Cros and Verlaine. He may briefly have met Rimbaud in the latter's company at a dinner that June. Only Hugo, newly returned from exile following the defeat of Napoleon III, remained a remote figure. Mallarmé would eventually be invited to his house in April 1878. But the main meeting-place for his own band of poets was the bookshop and publishing office in the Passage Choiseul, located just behind the Bibliothèque Nationale in the rue Richelieu and belonging to Alphonse Lemerre. The second volume of Lemerre's *Le Parnasse contemporain* had just appeared (already printed in 1869 but delayed by the war), and he would produce a third and final volume in 1876.

On 23 October 1872 one of the greatest of contemporary poets, Théophile Gautier, died. Glatigny immediately suggested to Banville that fellow poets should together revive the Renaissance tradition of the 'poetic tomb' and collaborate on a verse memorial; and the suggestion was taken up energetically by Gautier's son-in-law, Catulle Mendès. He envisaged not a collection of discrete works but one single, composite poem comprising a unified series of tributes, or 'toasts', given at an imaginary banquet, and he soon invited Mallarmé, among many others, to submit a contribution. He stipulated that each contribution should be approximately 60

lines long, in stanzaic form, beginning with a feminine rhyme
(a rhyme ending with an unvoiced 'e') and addressed overtly to
Gautier in the intimate 'tu' form.

Mallarmé fixed at once on the theme of Gautier the 'seer', and
'his mysterious gift of seeing with his eyes. (Delete "mysterious".)'
(*Corr.*, II. 37). The paradox that Mallarmé here adjusts by his
proposed deletion of 'mysterious' turns on his perception that
Gautier was not only literally a 'seer' – in that he was perhaps the
foremost art critic of his day – but also metaphorically a 'seer'.
This idea informs the resulting poem, 56 alexandrines in rhyming
couplets entitled 'Toast funèbre' (Funerary Toast), which was
incorporated in the *Tombeau de Théophile Gautier* published on the
first anniversary of Gautier's death. But Mallarmé complements
his tribute to Gautier's visionary abilities with an important, atheist
argument about how we should properly envisage the death of a
person. In the first section (after the required opening line addressing
the dead Gautier) the poet breaks with pious tradition by asserting
not that the departed lives on in our hearts and memories but that
he is well and truly dead. Here at this imaginary poetic symposium
he rejects the lesson of the Christian eucharist. As he raises his
glass of poetic tribute, he will not be saluting any conventional
notion of an afterlife or the risible prospect of some two-way
corridor along which the quick and the dead may come and go
as they please. A 'magic hope' of that kind smacks of 'madness',
and the wine of the eucharist is indeed, if so envisaged, a 'ghostly
libation'. No, the poet's chalice – and his poem – shall contain
only the 'golden monster!', the setting sun as symbol of the fact
and mystery of human mortality.

In the next two sections Mallarmé contrasts these two
fundamental responses to death. He ridicules the Christian view
by presenting a life lived in the hope of an afterlife as a form of
living death, the anguished perception (which had once made
da Vinci's Mona Lisa smile) that in life we are simply inadequate,

material versions of what we will eventually be in death. Gautier himself, however, exemplified a different kind of eucharist, the transubstantiation of poetry. With his 'penetrating eye' he has seen the world in such a way that the residual notion of a paradise is nevertheless saved and perpetuated by the sole agency of his poetic voice as it enacts the mystery of creation in naming the rose and the lily. For the truly immortal beauty of the rose and the lily derives not from those perennial flowers but from the everlasting linguistic entities created out of them: the wine-red rose and the chalice-shaped lily are the wherewithal of a poetic eucharist.

In the final section, in which the focus is once more on Gautier's tomb, the poet argues that the phenomena of the here and now ('the gardens of this star') impose an 'ideal duty': that is, a duty to perceive the *Idée*, to make out visual/mental forms amidst the contingent features of 'the Earth'. Accordingly he envisages the real tomb as the solid container of all that is inimical to this duty: 'avaricious silence' and 'massive night'. It is good that the tomb should lock in the negativity of death (timeless absence, darkness, wordlessness) so that the poetic tomb can better display the positive values of timeless presence, the sound of poetry, and the beauty of our visible and flower-bedecked world. And by containing many allusions to Gautier's own work, the poem serves in particular to 'resurrect' the poetic voice of the departed.

On 16 April 1873 Albert Glatigny, the poet and friend who had first published Mallarmé's prose poems and was himself recently widowed, died of tuberculosis at the age of 34, without seeing his brainchild, the *Tombeau de Théophile Gautier*, come into the world. On 5 September Ettie Maspero, née Yapp, died of puerperal fever five days after the birth of her second child. She was 27. Four years later Mallarmé would send her widower, the Egyptologist Gaston Maspero, a sonnet, dated on All Souls' Day, in which the now familiar argument is again put forward. On this occasion the poem is couched in the voice of the departed, who calls on her husband not to weigh her tomb down with flowers but rather to allow her spirit to rise up from it by murmuring her name by their fireside.

In an alternative form of resurrection the two women in whose company Mallarmé had first met Ettie at Fontainebleau reappeared in his life at this moment: Mme Gaillon and her daughter Nina de Villard. Their salon had been a meeting-place for future partisans of the Commune, and they had accordingly thought it wise to exile themselves temporarily to Geneva while the government got on with its reprisals. Now once more Nina became the cynosure of Bohemia, and it was in her salon that Mallarmé first met the most controversial painter of the day, Édouard Manet. The provocative treatment of female nudity and the overt debunking of two famous Renaissance masterpieces in *Le Déjeuner sur l'herbe* and *Olympia* (both painted in 1863, though the latter was not exhibited at the Salon until 1865) had brought him notoriety, as had the alleged 'unfinishedness' of his canvases. His studio was situated very near Mallarmé's apartment, and the poet soon took to dropping in regularly on the painter on his way home from school. They became close friends, with similar views on the need to place time-honoured artistic procedures and techniques at the service of a radically new, 'modern' perspective on the contemporary world. Through Manet Mallarmé met the novelist Émile Zola, an outspoken champion of Manet in the press during the 1860s and now embarked on his twenty-novel series *Les Rougon-Macquart*. Zola included him on the list of those to be sent *gratis* copies of each novel as it appeared, and in the ensuing years Mallarmé would scrupulously acknowledge receipt of these best-selling page-turners with a mixture of genuine approval (of Zola's visual imagination and his powerful, quasi-mythical transformations of the contemporary world) and courteously disguised critique (concerning the lack of suggestiveness in these novels, the absence of any 'dream-space' for the reader).

Through Manet Mallarmé was soon in contact with most of the leading young painters of Paris. When the following year they banded together to boycott the official Salon and mounted an exhibition in the studio of the photographer Nadar, a hostile critic dubbed their style of painting 'Impressionism'. Manet was ill-disposed to their confrontational tactics, but his own ability to upset the establishment at the École des Beaux-Arts persisted. When two of the paintings he submitted to that year's Salon were rejected, Mallarmé sprang to his defence in an article published in *La Renaissance littéraire et artistique*. Manet was currently the 'only man who has tried to open up a new path for himself and for painting' (*oc*, II. 414), he argued, denouncing the Salon selection committee for its reactionary distrust of his 'vision of the contemporary world' (*oc*, II. 412). Who were they to deny the exhibition-going public a chance to decide for itself? And, given the rapid evolution in Manet's radical choices of subject and treatment, why reject now what would soon seem tame?

The relationship between the two men deepened. Manet agreed to illustrate Mallarmé's translation of Poe's 'The Raven', and a fine-art edition appeared to favourable reviews under the

imprint of Lesclide in June 1875. Lemerre had rejected it, as he now rejected – on the advice of his selection panel of Banville, Coppée and Anatole France – the version of *L'Après-midi d'un faune* that Mallarmé had sent him for inclusion in the third volume of *Le Parnasse contemporain*. The poem, illustrated by Manet, was published instead by Derenne in April the following year. In that same year, in September, Mallarmé published a lengthy and well-informed article entitled 'The Impressionists and Édouard Manet' in *The Art Monthly Review* (written in French but translated into English by another). Here he introduced his British readership to Manet's innovative 'open air' painting, wonderfully exemplified in 'Le Linge' (The Washing), a photograph of which accompanied the article: 'in open air alone can the flesh tints of a model keep their true qualities, being nearly equally lighted on all sides' (*oc*, II. 455). For Manet the eye must see not what memory and custom make it believe it is seeing, but 'only that which it looks upon, and that as for the first time' (*oc*, II. 448); and in turn the painter will 'educate the public eye – as yet veiled by conventionality' (*oc*, II. 451). What the viewer sees in this new form of pictorial art, as in life, is a fleeting impression: 'the one thing needful is the time required by

Two of Édouard Manet's woodcut illustrations for Mallarmé's 1876 *L'Après-midi d'un faune*.

the spectator to see and admire the representation with that promptitude which just suffices for the connection of its truth' (*oc*, II. 457). And in this pioneering method Manet has shown the way to his pupil Éva Gonzalès, and to Monet, Sisley, Pissarro, Degas, Morisot and Cézanne. Just as the Pre-Raphaelites have sought inspiration by a return to the 'primitive simplicity of medieval ages', so 'the scope and aim . . . of Manet and his followers is that painting shall be steeped again in its cause, and its relation to nature' (*oc*, II. 469). In other words, painting is about colour, light and pattern, not mere obeisance to the Academy. For Mallarmé himself, of course, poetry needed similarly to be 'steeped' in its fundamental 'causes' – sound, meaning, structure – so that the word should appear every bit as unfamiliar ('as for the first time') as the visual phenomena depicted in a Manet painting. Doubtless this is why Hugo referred to him, not entirely favourably, as 'my dear Impressionist poet' when finally they met (*Corr.*, II. 170, n. 4). Manet responded to these supportive articles by painting his friend's portrait. He depicts him simply and intimately, the schoolteacher relaxing on a sofa during a visit to his studio, one hand in jacket pocket, the other holding a lighted cigar from which come curls of smoke that are perhaps suggestive of Mallarméan reveries and the dreamy spirals of their many conversations about art.

Manet's smoke rings might also have symbolized the whirls and eddies of his friend's immersion in the cultural and journalistic life of Paris and London. Charles Wendelen, a close neighbour at 34 rue de Moscou, ran a journal called *La Dernière Mode. Gazette du monde et de la famille*, which published colour-plates and patterns of the latest dress fashions. Mallarmé saw a chance to leave the class-room behind by building on his experiences in South Kensington. Fortnightly, from 6 September 1874, he added word to silent image and filled the magazine with his own copy. Under a variety of playful pseudonyms that suggested an extensive list of contributors (Mme Margurite de Ponty, Miss Satin, A Creole Lady, the Chief

Édouard Manet, *Stéphane Mallarmé*, 1876, oil on canvas.

Taster at Brébant's restaurant, Ix – i.e. 'neuf', meaning 'nine' but also 'new'), the initiate of Nothingness wrote all manner of articles on the material world and indeed on the world of materials: costume and fashion, jewellery, millinery, furniture, interior decoration, cookery (with recipes and sample menus), travel. To these he added regular columns: 'Advice on Education'; a 'Chronicle of Paris' that included his own brief reviews of plays, books, concerts, exhibitions, etc.; poems, songs, and stories submitted by his friends; and a letters section replete with the contributions of wholly imaginary correspondents.

La Dernière Mode is an extraordinary publication, part serious journal, part spoof, part crash course for an innovative prose stylist, and part verbal orgy of naming. The man who had nearly lost his wits in contemplating the yawning chasm between words and things seems here intent on an allopathic celebration of the ability of language to describe the physical world down to the very last button.

SEPTIEME LIVRAISON   DIMANCHE 6 DECEMBRE 1874

Paraît le 1ᵉʳ et le 3ᵉ Dimanche du mois, avec le Concours

DANS LA MODE ET LE GOUT PARISIEN

DES GRANDES FAISEUSES, DE TAPISSIERS-DÉCORATEURS, DE MAITRES QUEUX DE JARDINIERS, D'AMATEURS DE BIBELOTS ET DU SPORT

EN MUSIQUE

DES PRINCIPAUX COMPOSITEURS

EN LITTÉRATURE

DE THÉODORE DE BANVILLE, LÉON CLADEL, FRANÇOIS COPPÉE, ALPHONSE DAUDET, LÉON DIERX, EMMANUEL DES ESSARTS, ERNEST D'HERVILLY, ALBERT MÉRAT, STÉPHANE MALLARMÉ, CATULLE MENDÈS, SULLY PRUDHOMME, LÉON VALADE, AUGUSTE VILLIERS DE L'ISLE ADAM, ÉMILE ZOLA, ETC.

Toilette de Bal et Toilette de Théâtre ou de Concert.

Title-page of an issue of *La Dernière Mode*.

Yet, just as in thinking about language Mallarmé had wondered at the relationship between the eternal Word and its time-bound manifestations in particular languages, and just as in assessing the London Exhibitions he had been seen objects (brand new or antique) as embodying the passage of time, so too here he sees the solar drama at work in the rise and fall of fashions and the annual rhythms of the cultural 'seasons'. The ephemerality of the latest thing belies an eternal cyclicity. Flares, like the sun, are sometimes in and sometimes out.

For four months Mallarmé cannot have slept but he must surely have had fun. In January 1875, however, the magazine changed hands, unbeknownst to its principal contributor, who wrote a circular letter to his friends in outrage: 'I've been robbed of several months' hard work' (*Corr.*, ii. 52). He told them to have nothing to do with the new management, and indeed the journal ceased publication in May. Meanwhile in March the Mallarmés moved to a fourth-floor flat in the nearby rue de Rome (at 87, later re-numbered 89) – away from Wendelen, and much closer to Manet.

In the summer holidays of 1875 Marie took Vève and Anatole to see her father and sister in Camberg, just as she had done two years earlier. On that occasion her husband had escaped to the coast of Brittany to do some writing. This time he went to London for a fortnight in August. He had plans to publish an edition of *Vathek*, a Gothic novel by William Beckford. Beckford had written this in French in the early 1780s, but the novel had appeared first in an English translation (1786). Since its publication in French in 1787 the novel had been largely forgotten in France, and Mallarmé wanted to present its merits in a preface, thereby 'restoring it to French Literature' (*Corr.*, ii. 119). He was keen to consult a copy of the rare first French edition at the British Museum. Here, through John Payne, he met fellow poets and writers who were also members of its staff, notably Arthur O'Shaughnessy, francophile poet and vigorous promoter of the Parnassians in England, and also various members of the Pre-Raphaelite group, including Ford Madox Brown, and possibly William Morris and Dante Gabriel Rossetti. He certainly met Walter Pater, the Oxford academic, writer and art critic – and would do so again much later on his lecture visit to Oxford in 1894.

Since Marie and the children would be in Germany till the end of September Mallarmé stopped off at Equihen, near Boulogne, on his way home. Manet had recommended it, and here he could write (probably *Les Mots anglais*). But full board and lodging were not cheap, and once again he found himself in financial difficulty. He might even have to pawn his watch just to be able to send Marie and the children money for their fares home. But they were soon reunited without such measures, and the school year began once more. This time, instead of writing for *La Dernière Mode*, Mallarmé had secured a contract with *The Athenaeum*, one of the foremost weekly arts journals in Britain: he was to supply it with regular short articles – to be published anonymously as 'Gossips' – about the latest events in the cultural life of Paris. He would submit his copy in French, and O'Shaughnessy, who had secured the contract for him, would translate them. Mallarmé's first contribution appeared on 6 November 1875, and his last on 1 April 1876: his persistent championing of Manet had finally exhausted the editor's patience. But Mallarmé continued to correspond with O'Shaughnessy, and to welcome him and his writer-wife, Eleanor Marston, to the rue de Rome whenever they visited Paris. It was a blow, therefore, when Eleanor died in January 1879 (Marie had liked her greatly), and another when O'Shaughnessy himself died two years later of pneumonia in January 1881, aged 36. Their two infant children had predeceased them.

Now in his early to mid-thirties the poet-cum-journalist-cum-teacher-cum-breadwinner was leading the busiest of lives, and his correspondence echoes with happy complaint about how hard-pressed he is. He has articles to write, forthcoming books to proof-read, gatherings to attend. But while journalism helped to pay the bills, the real focus of Mallarmé's literary effort at this time appears to have been an ambitious project for the theatre. In January 1876 he tells O'Shaughnessy that as well as putting the finishing touches to his 'playlet' about the Faun he is also preparing a major theatrical work: 'for it is possible that I shall be producing nothing but plays for several years now so as to acquire the freedom to write other, lyrical verse' (*Corr.*, II. 101). In February and March he is working hard on 'a great big popular melodrama' (*Corr.*, II. 103; II. 105; II. 108). By the following January this has become 'a drama to be performed at fixed periodic intervals' (*Corr.*, II. 144), as though he were envisaging something like the Oberammagau Passion Play or perhaps a 'Ring cycle' to match the seasons of the year. And by May he is talking of his 'vast theatrical labour', of 'the great endeavour of an entirely new form of theatre' that will 'take him several years': a triple drama, at once 'magical, popular and lyrical' (*Corr.*, II. 151) – in other words, a quasi-Wagnerian 'total work of art', like the Ring itself, first performed at Bayreuth in the summer of 1876.

Meanwhile Mallarmé was helping to found a new review. Lemerre's recent publishing decisions (from which Leconte de Lisle and Verlaine had suffered as well as himself) led the 'Parnassians' to seek new outlets for their work, and in Alphonse Derenne, hitherto noted for his publication of theses on obstetrics, they found a willing midwife. In December 1875 the first issue of *La République des Lettres* appeared, and was soon vaunted in Mallarmé's 'Gossips' as 'a strictly and purely literary magazine' (*oc*, II. 429). Mallarmé had played a key role in the negotiations with Derenne, together with Mendès and Henri Roujon, the writer and future director of the École des Beaux-Arts; and he contributed two prose poems to its first issue: 'Le Phénomène futur' (The Freak of the Future), written in Tournon, and a new one, 'Un spectacle interrompu' (A Spectacle Interrupted), in which the first-person voice is that of a self-appointed 'reporter' whose duty is to 'remark events in a light appropriate to dream' (*oc*, I. 240).

The review prided itself not only on the quality of its French contributors – featuring many established writers such as Flaubert, Banville and Leconte de Lisle, as well as rising stars like Zola (*L'Assommoir* appeared here first in serial form from July 1876, when the hitherto monthly review became a Sunday weekly) – but also on its international character. The inaugural issue included a poem in French by Swinburne, the second a piece by Turgenev. Swinburne in particular, already the grateful recipient of a copy of the Mallarmé–Manet version of *The Raven*, was enthusiastic, and offered a further poem in French for the third issue. And it was through Swinburne's intervention (seconded by the leading Poe scholar, John H. Ingram) that Mallarmé was now invited to contribute to a memorial volume currently being prepared in honour of Poe by Sigourney Rice. She had recently chaired the committee that secured the erection of a physical memorial to Poe in Westminster Church in Baltimore and was planning a more literary 'tomb' to accompany it. In July Mallarmé submitted a draft version of his celebrated sonnet 'Le Tombeau d'Edgar Poe' to Sarah Helen Whitman, Poe's former fiancée, in his own English translation; and in December 1876 he sent Sigourney Rice the French version, which appeared the following year in *E. Allan Poe: A Memorial Volume*.

Like 'Toast funèbre' the poem contains many allusions to its subject's work (and to Baudelaire's well-known essay on him), and presents itself as an attempt – by linguistic means – to put a stop to all the 'blasphemy' (etymologically, bad talk, or bad-mouthing) to which Poe has been subject since his death (being accused in particular as a worthless alcoholic). Instead the poem offers itself as an adornment of Poe's tomb that will celebrate the writer's 'angelic' capacity to 'give a purer meaning to the words of the tribe'. 'Tel qu'en Lui-même enfin l'éternité le change', the sonnet famously begins: as into Himself at last eternity changes him. In death Poe the human being has become Poe the Poet, truly and eternally Himself.

After his first few years at the Lycée Condorcet Mallarmé had begun to neglect his teaching duties again, and the reports on him by the headmaster and the school inspector in the mid-'70s suggest that he was in danger of being banished once more to the provinces. It was therefore important that he demonstrate his pedagogical talents – or provide for his family financially in the event of dismissal – by publishing as soon as possible the two school manuals that he had been working on and which would eventually appear as *Les Mots anglais* (English Words) in December 1877 and *Les Dieux antiques* in December 1879. Come the summer of 1876 he despatched his wife and children to Valvins, where the family had first stayed in the summer of 1874, while he himself returned to the coast of Normandy for a month before joining them in September. In subsequent summers, however, and at other points in the school year whenever possible, Valvins would become his favourite refuge, noisy children or no noisy children: he found its riverside location a great source of peace and inspiration.

Les Mots anglais is subtitled 'A Short Philology for Use in the Classroom and by the General Public' and was intended as the first of two volumes, of which the second (never published) would have been concerned with the rules of English grammar. This first volume is principally an account of the history of the English language in terms of its lexis, and relies heavily on Chambers's *Etymological Dictionary of the English Language* (1874) and John Earle's recently published *The Philology of the English Tongue* (1871; 2nd edn, 1873). Its overt emphasis is on the rich plurality of the English language, fed by the twin streams of Anglo-Saxon and the French of the Norman conquerors, but it is also the work of a poet who is fascinated by the relationship between words and things. In particular the teacher–poet seems to espouse the Cratylist idea of a direct co-relation between particular sounds and particular material phenomena, finding in each initial consonant 'something like the fundamental meaning of the word [it begins]' (*oc*, II. 1016). In part this is a mnemonic device, grouping words that begin with the same letter and imprinting them in the memory by a supposed communality of meaning (e.g. 'K' betokens knottedness, juncture). But in part also it derives from the view, derived from Max Müller and others, that linguistic usage and linguistic change are determined by unconscious procedures, here that of alliteration, that are inherently poetic in nature.

The publication of *Les Mots anglais* (by Truchy, a publisher of textbooks) allowed Mallarmé's influential friend, Charles Seignobos, to argue that its author was eligible for promotion on the pay scale, and his annual salary was duly increased to 4,200 francs. In the course of 1878 and 1879 Mallarmé signed contracts for further textbooks, receiving welcome advances on royalties: 300 francs for *Ce que c'est que l'anglais* (What English Is); 600 francs for *Thèmes anglais*, a grammar and translation exercise book that also provided well-known phrases and proverbs (from a recently published *Handbook of Proverbs*) as an aide-mémoire for the student; and 1,000 francs for an anthology to be entitled *The Beauties of English Prose and Rhyme*. This trilogy was to have constituted a 'Complete English Course in Three Volumes', but, while extensive manuscripts survive of each of its three parts, none was ever published. (*Les Mots anglais* had not done well.) Similarly an advance of 600 francs for a translation of *New English Mercantile Correspondence* was never honoured: business English was even less the poet's forte. An anthology of English nursery rhymes was also mooted, and Mallarmé plundered Walter Crane's *Baby's Bouquet* (1879) and Kate Greenaway's *Mother Goose or the Old Nursery Rhymes* (1881) for the purpose: but this project, too, was aborted. Likewise a passing notion to translate *A Child's History of England*, by Charles Dickens.

With all these advances Mallarmé was temporarily very well off, and in the summer of 1878 he bought Vève and Anatole a child's carriage and hired a pony to take them on long excursions through the forest of Fontainebleau. He also acquired a small boat, which he christened the *Vève*. The two-month school holiday in August and September was spent *en famille* at Valvins. In the spring of 1879, however, seven-year-old Anatole fell ill with a recurrence of the

Mallarmé's son Anatole in an unsigned, undated oil painting.

rheumatic condition that had plagued him since birth (and had killed his grandmother and aunt). Marie remained behind in Paris to tend her son as her husband took Vève down to a rather chilly Valvins. On their return it was clear that the boy's condition had worsened: the valves of his heart were affected. The new-found wealth had to be spent on expensive medical experts, but they were powerless. Cazalis, now a doctor, tried to offer reassurance. Come June there seemed to be some improvement, but as the boy turned eight in July his health deteriorated further: fluid retention was a symptom of the disease, and his stomach was horribly swollen.

In August a new acquaintance of Mallarmé's, the comte Robert de Montesquiou, gave the boy a resplendent budgerigar, which brought him considerable pleasure. As a grateful Mallarmé informed the donor, the bird had been christened Sémiramis, because she was like 'a fairytale princess held captive in a fairytale palace', and because her plumage reflected the 'jewelled gardens' of her prison (*Corr.*, ii. 197). The family took the 'princess' with them to Valvins, judging that Anatole was well enough to travel and that the climate at Valvins would be good for him. The comte, a renowned dandy and aesthete, was to become famous as the presumed model for the figure of Des Esseintes in Huysmans' novel *À rebours* (1884) and later for the Baron de Charlus in Proust's *À la recherche du temps perdu*. For the moment, however, he took an entirely unadorned and sincerely felt interest in the young child's plight. The days and weeks were punctuated by the twin poles of crisis and remission. A milk diet was prescribed, but steadily the condition worsened. Attempts were made to drain fluid from the stomach. Mallarmé himself began to accept that the outcome was inevitable, but kept his thoughts from his wife.

At the beginning of October the start of the school year meant a return to Paris. The exertions of the journey and a ceaseless cough weakened the boy further, and on Tuesday, 7 October, Mallarmé wrote in some despair to his friend, John Payne: 'this charming, exquisite child had captivated me to such a degree that I see him in all my future projects and in my dearest dreams' (*Corr.*, II. 201). Past, present, and future: the most critical of critical moments. At three o'clock that afternoon, while Mallarmé was out posting this letter and another, to Robert de Montesquiou, Anatole died. Stéphane, Marie and Vève returned with his body to Valvins, to bury him in the cemetery just up river at Samoreau, where they would later join him. Past, present, and future: mother, sister, son, now all dead.

5

Tuesdays

In the weeks leading up to Anatole's death Mallarmé had hesitated to tell his correspondents that his son's illness was probably terminal. To have done so, he thought, would have seemed like hastening that inevitable outcome himself. Now, as he tried to write his way through his grief, he found himself faced with a similar reluctance: to mark this death with a literary work of art, as he had the deaths of Gautier and Poe, would be to confirm it, to accept it. But he could not countenance a 'moral burial' of this kind: 'Oh! this sacrifice – for that to deny his life – to bury him – let us talk about him some more, evoke him – in reality, silence.' The extensive, fragmentary notes that bear poignant witness to this attempt (*oc*, I. 513–45) reveal the conflicting currents of guilt, outrage and regret that fuelled this grief and this reluctance.

'Never knew mother, son never knew me!': an angry sense of generational interruption runs strongly through the notes, as though the natural order of things had been profoundly upset. Indeed time has been reversed, with the son predeceasing his father and mother. The father feels it as a duty to 'perpetuate' his son ('it's me, the man you would have been') while somehow dying himself: 'no more *life* for me and I can feel myself laid out in the tomb beside you'. Likewise a perfect symmetry has been shattered: 'equilibrium father son mother daughter broken – three, a void between us, searching'. The father, 'cursing his blood' and the 'hereditary illness in me', does not 'dare endure this gaze full of

Anatole, aged 7 or 8, wearing the sailor suit in which he was buried and which figures as a poignant image in the 'Notes for *Anatole's Tomb*'.

the future'. He tries desperately, as in 'Toast funèbre', to deny the importance of a physical absence, and he wants to treasure instead the 'spiritual' survival of the departed in the thoughts and loving remembrance of the living: 'he is nothing but spirit in us now . . . death powerless against human genius so long as humanity'. But vivid memories of his son keep returning, and he thinks sadly of the sailor suit in which they buried him: 'little sailor – with your suit on / eh? – for a great crossing / a wave swept you away / sea, ascites'. 'Ascites', or dropsy of the abdomen, recalls the fluid retention that had so discomfited and disfigured Anatole in his dying days. It is here transformed into the tsunami of mortality in a poetic image that seems clumsy and grotesque. This time art cannot perpetuate life: the solar drama has stalled.

One of the first notes jotted down by Anatole's grieving father shows his characteristic mindset: 'Ill in spring dead in autumn – it's the sun'. It was therefore by a sad irony that *Les Dieux antiques*, his translation-cum-adaptation of George Cox's *Manual of Mythology*, should appear two months later. Just as *Les Mots anglais* grew out of Mallarmé's erstwhile ambition to write a doctoral thesis about language, so *Les Dieux antiques* may correspond to 'De divinitate', the compulsory subsidiary thesis in Latin that he had also once envisaged. In *Les Dieux antiques* Mallarmé maintains Cox's categories and subdivisions but abandons his question-and-answer format, recasting the content as affirmative narrative and adding his own explicit and implicit emphases. Cox was popularizing Max Müller's thesis that myth is the product of unconscious linguistic processes, and that ancient myths are the fossilized versions of an original myth about the passage of the sun and can be revealed as such by precise etymological study. For Müller and Cox the hidden agenda was to demonstrate a universal religious model of which the Christian religion offered – in the resurrection of Jesus – the most authentic and powerful manifestation. But Mallarmé seeks to subvert this agenda by consistently translating 'God' by 'divinité', meaning less a divinity than the quality of 'divinity', which for him is what we call the unknowable and project onto the heavens above. Accordingly he sees it as the work of poets consciously to create new 'fables' with which to offer solace to the anguished human mind. Thus in May 1879 he had written to Leconte de Lisle, author of *Poèmes antiques* and *Poèmes barbares*, to ask his permission to cite some of his verse at the end of his forthcoming publication in order to show his intended young audience just what a 'magnificent and living continuation' of this tradition of 'fable' is evident in the work of contemporary writers (*oc*, I. 779). And in a section of his opening chapter on the 'Origin and Development of Mythology' Mallarmé as translator notes the need for a future study that will demonstrate the 'capricious transformations' of the solar drama that have found expression in the 'fables' of many earlier poets also.

Mallarmé would later dismiss *Les Mots anglais* and *Les Dieux antiques* as mere potboilers, but it is clear that their subject matter is very closely implicated in his own ambitions as a poet. With increasing concertedness he now envisaged a form of writing, of modern mythology, that would figure 'Nature's Tragedy' (Müller's phrase for the sunset and the human mortality that it symbolizes) from a contemporary perspective, articulating and perhaps allaying our deep-seated fears through the subliminal power of poetic rhythm and the 'musical' relationships of the *Idée*.

For the moment, however, he was wordless with grief. And ill. In May and June 1880, as though acting on his expressed desire to be his son's heir, he suffered a severe attack of the same rheumatic disease and was bedridden for the whole of May and June. A further month's sick leave and the two-month school holidays spent at Valvins brought some relief. On 8 October Mallarmé and his wife marked the first anniversary of Anatole's death, and soon afterwards he wrote to his stepsister Jeanne Michaud about how this constituted 'a new separation': 'it closes a cycle of moments in which we were able to say to each other: "A year ago our darling boy was still alive, he was doing this or that . . ."' (*Corr.*, II. 212). Come December he was still not fully recovered, and his teaching schedule continued to be disrupted by his absences. Marie, meanwhile, continued to grieve, for Anatole and for her own father who had died in April that year. Her stomach problems persisted worryingly, and she seemed now to have nothing to live for. Her daughter would soon be an adult, her son was gone, and her husband appeared to live only for poetry. As he once had, so she too now came to know the twin chasms of Nothingness and ill health. But she found no solace in writing.

In January 1881 Mallarmé describes himself in a letter as 'living more and more apart, and immersed in a major project of several years' standing' (*Corr.*, II. 220). The addressee was Gustave Kahn, seventeen years his junior and one of the new generation of poets that was about to provoke the literary world with its *vers libre* (free verse), its 'Symbolism' and its 'Decadence'. Kahn and his fellow poet Jules Laforgue were admirers of Mallarmé's work, and Kahn had recently plucked up courage to pay the Master a visit in the rue de Rome. Now, however, he was away on military service in Algeria and avid for news from home. All a reclusive Mallarmé could manage was a somewhat mixed set of comments on Flaubert's posthumously published novel, *Bouvard et Pécuchet*.

But gradually Mallarmé was beginning to resume contact with the literary and cultural world of Paris. As he put it to Verlaine in the same month, 'I still exist on Tuesday evenings' (*Corr.*, II. 221). For a number of years Mallarmé had been in the habit of holding open house on Tuesday evenings, between 9 and 11 o'clock. Guests, women as well as men, could come and go as they pleased in this middle-class version of a salon. In the Mallarmés' exiguous living-cum-dining-room, the end of the Louis Quatorze dining-table was folded down to create space, a Chinese pot full of tobacco was placed upon it, together with cigarette papers for non-pipe-smokers, the overhead gaslamp was covered in crepe to dim the light, and Marie and Geneviève would make ready to serve grog to the assembled party. They would customarily withdraw from the proceedings at 10 o'clock. Originally Tuesdays had been Thursdays, but Zola had commandeered that day. Mendès and Augusta Holmès had Wednesdays and Fridays, while Heredia had Saturday afternoons and Leconte de Lisle Saturday evenings. Banville seemed to prefer Sundays. No matter the day, the advantage of this arrangement for Mallarmé was that he could enjoy the company of like-minded people without deserting his wife and daughter. Familiar friends – Cazalis, Villiers (spasmodically),

Pierre Louÿs's sketch of the layout of Mallarmé's apartment during the period of the *mardis*, with indications of where Mallarmé would stand by the stove and where Marie and Geneviève Mallarmé, Whistler, and he himself would sit.

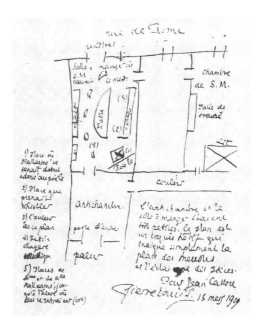

Mendès, Verlaine (rarely), Roujon – mixed with newer, younger figures, like Kahn and Laforgue.

Mallarmé's *mardis* became more famous than any of its weekday alternatives, and endured for the rest of his life (when he was not at Valvins) as the one Parisian gathering to which any ambitious young writer or artist – or cultural tourist – sought admission. Like secular vespers, or a séance with the living, attended by the resident cat and illuminated by the solar symbol of the gas-lamp above the table of smoker's requisites, a Mallarméan *mardi* was itself, of course, a form of arcane drama, his living-room a theatre in which the officiating host could orchestrate discussion in alternating periods of vatic monologue, hospitable dialogue, and sybilline silence.

Another form of drama occupied Mallarmé's attention that summer at Valvins. He had remained in close touch with Eudoxie Margueritte, a first cousin on his father's side and some three years older than himself. Recently widowed by the Franco-Prussian War and the mother of two sons, Paul and Victor, she had rented a house for the holidays at Samois, just downriver from Valvins on the opposite bank. In a former attic workshop above a large barn, with a splendid view over the Seine, her sons proceeded to create a makeshift theatre. Each Sunday the temporary benches would fill with friends and other locals: M. et Mme Prosper Mary, owners of the house in which Mallarmé lived and occupants of its ground floor; M. et Mme Aubert, owners of the Auberge des Rosiers next door to it; Léopold Dauphin, poet and composer, with his wife Marguerite, great friends ever since the Mallarmés had first come to Valvins seven years earlier; Jean Marras, now keeper at the nearby Palais de Fontainbleau and a friend of Mallarmé, Mendès and Villiers since the 1860s; Henry Roujon and his German wife Madeleine (with whom Marie Mallarmé could speak her native language). As soon as the local mayor gave the nod, the proceedings began: perhaps an old farce or some *commedia dell'arte* routines, but also Hugo's famous Romantic drama *Hernani*, and works by Coppée and Banville. Geneviève Mallarmé often took the leading female role, and with great success. Offers of marriage ensued . . . and were rebuffed.

Enlisted as adviser, occasional director, and trusty prompter, Mallarmé participated with the attentive interest of one who had been working on a 'popular melodrama' for the past decade and whose work is laced with reminiscences of the circus visit that he and his sister had enjoyed in the company of Aunt Herminie. Popular spectacle had always fascinated him, like that depicted in 'Un spectacle interrompu' (1875). Witness also his letter to O'Shaughnessy in December 1877 where he talks of creating a new form of theatre that will 'dazzle the sovereign people' and reserve a special role for the American acrobat and dancer Leona Dare, currently wowing her audiences at the Folies-Bergère (*Corr.*, II. 159). The mime work of these summer thespians was also of particular

Paul Verlaine's pen-and-ink drawing of Mallarmé during one of his *mardis*.

Participants in the theatricals at Valvins (1881–82), including Geneviève Mallarmé seated on the right.

interest to a poet increasingly interested in writing as a form of silent action on the page, and Paul Marguerrite was an effective mime artist. When this informal Théâtre de Valvins reopened for its summer season the following year, Paul performed the mime *Pierrot sceptique*, written by the novelist and art critic Joris-Karl Huysmans. Inspired by the role and by a couplet from Gautier, Paul then wrote his own mime, *Pierrot assassin de sa femme*, in which – to a musical accompaniment – Pierrot returns from Columbine's funeral and commits suicide by tickling himself to death in a mimed re-enactment of his earlier murder of his wife. First performed on 15 September 1882 this mime was immediately published: it would intrigue Mallarmé for some time to come, not least when it was performed (and republished) in Paris four years later.

Mallarmé shared this interest in popular culture with Manet, who was then working on his famous painting *Un bar aux Folies-Bergère*. Learning that others were planning to publish a book of Poe's poems in translation Mallarmé sought Manet's collaboration once more for an illustrated edition of his own translations (which he had been publishing piecemeal in periodicals over recent years). Manet agreed, but his health was failing: hardening arteries and circulatory problems eventually led to gangrene, amputation and, on 30 April 1883, death. Mallarmé felt the loss keenly, of a soul-mate whom he had visited so regularly on his way home from school and of a painter with whose work he felt so closely in tune. He would seek solace the following year in multiple visits to the Manet retrospective at the École des Beaux-Arts.

The loss of Manet brought him another soulmate, however, as though the cyclicity of the solar drama were indeed dictating the rhythms of his personal attachments: a soulmate and perhaps, briefly, a mistress. Anne Rose Suzanne Louviot, of illegitimate birth, had at the age of fifteen married a 27-year-old grocer in Nancy, Jean-Claude Laurent, who soon went bust and from whom she separated before her sixteenth birthday. (Divorce, first legalized in France in 1792, was abolished in 1816 and re-established only in July 1884.) It is possible that this marriage was arranged to legitimate a pregnancy initiated by the 55-year-old military governor of Nancy, and that the child was consigned to an orphanage. Once in Paris, and taking her mother's Christian name, Marie Laurent became an actress, displaying her tall, statuesque beauty, her golden hair, and her well-developed figure on the Parisian stage until she was spotted by Dr Thomas W. Evans, the wealthy American dentist who numbered the Emperor Napoléon III among his clients. Evans established his new mistress – Méry (reflecting the anglophone Mary) Laurent – in an apartment at 52 rue de Rome, and subsequently provided her with a small house, Les Talus, on the edge of the Bois de Boulogne as her summer residence. She would become the principal model for Proust's Odette de Crécy.

A photographic *carte de visite* of Méry Laurent, *c.* 1870s.

But first, since 1876, she had been Manet's model, sitting for him at his nearby studio in the rue de Rome – and sleeping with him. Through Manet she met many of his friends, including Mallarmé. Did she sleep with the Faun also? The question remains largely moot. Huysmans later noted in a diary that she denied having done so, citing reasons pertaining to the poet's personal hygiene and standards of dress. No incontrovertible evidence is to be obtained either way from the correspondence that they exchanged over the next fifteen years. Mallarmé burnt her letters to him, while a legal embargo prevented his letters to her from being published until 1996, almost a century after Méry's death (in 1900). The embargo itself, however, may speak volumes. The tone of the correspondence varies, often no doubt because some of the letters have been written in the knowledge that they may be seen by other eyes. But Mallarmé begins to use the intimate 'tu' form from midway through 1888 and thereafter addresses Méry frequently as 'chérie'. In the summers of 1888 and 1889 he accepted an invitation to join her and Dr Evans in the spa town of Royat in the Auvergne, where he took the waters in their company. This period may have marked the most intimate period of their relationship, for Mallarmé's letter to Méry of 11 September 1889 does suggest that she has, the previous winter, ended a physical relationship between them: he tells her of the difficulty he is having – and has just been enduring at Royat – in continuing to see her so frequently on the simple basis of their 'good, long-standing friendship'.

Be this as it may, after Manet's death Mallarmé found particular comfort in Méry's vivacious and ever-cheerful company and drew stimulus from her genuine and knowledgeable interest in the arts. They remained firm friends during the remainder of his life. Her taste for display and her enthusiasm for the fashionable accessory of the fan may explain the affectionate nickname of Paon (Peacock) that he gave her, for the poems that she inspired (including three sonnets, a rondel, a song and other pieces of occasional verse) include reference to her coquettish deployment of this fan(tail) to disguise – and, of course, thereby suggest – the imminent possibility of a warm laugh or even a kiss. He now began to visit her regularly after school, as once he had Manet, and her drawing-room – in the rue de Rome or at Les Talus – was always a place in which he could be sure to meet their mutual friends and raise his spirits. How different this was from the sad silence of his own home, the 'morose interior' (*Corr.*, ii. 250) where Marie's depression was casting its grim pall – a depression increased by her husband's unconcealed delight in his new friend.

Among the rising generation of poets, like Kahn and Laforgue, Mallarmé was an enigmatic figure. It was becoming increasingly difficult even to obtain access to his work. He had not published any poem since *L'Après-midi d'un faune* (1876), and copies of this collector's item were in any case impossible to obtain. Responding to an approach from the editor of Lutèce, a recently relaunched review, Verlaine undertook to write a series of articles under the ambiguous title of *Les Poètes maudits*. (Are poets perhaps 'cursed' less by fate than by their hostile readers?) His first article was devoted to Tristan Corbière, who had published a collection of black-humoured verse, *Les Amours jaunes* (Yellow Loves), in 1873 before dying of tuberculosis at the age of 29. His second article, unsurprisingly, was about Rimbaud. Mallarmé was next. Verlaine wrote to him in August 1883 requesting a photograph and permission to reprint some of his early verse. Nervously Mallarmé agreed, wondering how his early work would look alongside the innovations of Corbière and Rimbaud. In November, while he was having a photograph of his portrait by Manet taken for the purpose, another letter came, asking if possible for some unpublished material. Verlaine was short of copy. Mallarmé explained that 'despite one of the greatest literary labours ever attempted', he had no *new* unpublished verse to hand: 'I am busy with the armature of my work, which is in prose. We [poets] have all been so behind in respect of our thinking that I've spent no less than ten years elaborating mine' (*Corr.*, II. 248).

The finished article began to appear later that month, in three weekly instalments. Verlaine presents his friend predominantly as the poet of the first and second volumes of *Le Parnasse contemporain*, a kind of exquisite whose scandalous obscurity was attacked and lampooned by critical opinion. Like Corbière and Rimbaud, he argues, Mallarmé also suffered from 'la malédiction', another doomed victim of badmouthing. Verlaine pads out his commentary by mentioning various other works by Mallarmé and ends with a flourish: 'He is working on a book whose profundity will astound every bit as much as its brilliance will dazzle all but the blind. But when, dear friend, when?' His 'dear friend' was disappointed by the vacuousness of this article and regretted these counterproductive reminders of the hostile reception to which his poetry had once been subject – and perhaps always would be.

Two years later Verlaine began a similar but much longer series of articles, under the heading of *Les Hommes d'aujourd'hui*, in which he introduced to the French reading public some 29 'men of today', almost all poets and writers. This time, at Verlaine's request and perhaps with a view to improving the eventual article, Mallarmé provided him with some personal information: about his ancestry and youth, about his current life and growing celebrity, and about the Great Work. This famous letter contains these much-quoted words:

Beyond the prose pieces and the poems of my youth and those that followed, echoing them, and which were published here and there every time the first issue of some Literary Review appeared, I have always dreamt of and striven for something else, with the patience of an alchemist, ready to sacrifice all vanity and gratification to it the way people used to burn their furniture and even the beams in their roof to feed the furnace of the Great Work. What exactly? It is difficult to say: a book, quite simply, in several volumes, a book that is a book, architectural and premeditated, and not a collection of random inspirations, however marvellous . . . I shall go further and say: the Book, persuaded as I am that ultimately there is only one, attempted unwittingly by anyone who has ever written, even writers of genius. The Orphic explanation of the Earth, which is the only duty of the poet and the literary game *par excellence*; for the very rhythm of the book, impersonal and living, even in its pagination, aligns itself with the equations of this dream, or Ode. There you have it, the confession of my vice laid bare, dear friend, a vice I have a thousand times rejected, my spirit bruised or weary, but the whole thing possesses me and I shall perhaps succeed: not in completing this work in its entirety (one would need to be I know not who to manage that!) but in displaying one finished fragment of it, to make one corner of its glorious authenticity shine forth like a star, while implying the whole of the remainder for which a single life is not enough. To prove by the parts completed that this book exists, and that I have known that which I could not accomplish. (*oc*, I. 788)

It is sometimes argued that this letter presents a carefully wrought and not wholly reliable self-image that Mallarmé hoped to see Verlaine pass on to the world at large. Yet its thrust and content are perfectly genuine. Fundamentally it is the account of a *writer*. Hence Mallarmé's playful highlighting of his writerly ancestors: the penpushers in the Enregistrement, but also the official in the censorship department under Louis XVI whose name he discovered on the title-page of the first French edition of Beckford's *Vathek*. In response to Verlaine's challenge in *Les Poètes maudits* he explains that the Great Work – the Book – is a real objective but difficult, indeed impossible, to achieve. And he elaborates. This work will be 'anonymous, the Text speaking for itself and without an authorial voice' (*oc*, I. 789). Here he is recalling his now longstanding conception of the poem as a quasi-theatrical stage on which language performs, generating its own 'myths'.

The growing sense of the 'impossibility' of the task derives from his similarly longstanding ambition for a text that will somehow 'say it all', that will embody and orchestrate the 'pure rhythmic motifs of being' (what he had earlier termed the 'Universe'). This is presumably why from the start Mallarmé had wanted to complete the whole – 'architectural and premeditated' – before publishing any part. Hence, in this letter to Verlaine, Mallarmé's dismissive tone concerning what he has published so far and the possibility of future 'selections' of his work, in which publishers are beginning to show an interest. The opposite of the Book is the 'album' – a 'condemnatory word' – and while he does accept the possibility of bringing out an *Album de vers et de prose* (as he indeed would in Brussels in 1887), this is a side-line. In fact publishing for a contemporary readership is a diversion, something to be done perhaps out of a kind of courtesy but a potentially fatal distraction all the same:

> Ultimately I consider the contemporary epoch to be an interregnum for the poet, and it is not his business to get mixed up in it: the epoch is too full of desuetude and too full of preparatory effervescence for him to have any other course of action but to work away mysteriously with a view to later – or never – and occasionally to send the living his visiting card – some stanzas or a sonnet – so as not to be stoned by them if they were to suspect him of knowing that they do not exist / have no place/ are not happening [n'ont pas lieu].

The wry humour, the concision and the wordplay are characteristic of a Mallarmé whose prose style was no less radical and no less effective than his verse. He had said much the same back in his very first letter to Verlaine in December 1866 (*Corr.*, I. 235–7), but how much more subtly he expressed it now in 1885.

It is the writer, too, who acknowledges that he has published potboilers like *Les Mots anglais* and *Les Dieux antiques*, but he has a family to support – and a 'ruinous' passion for boating to indulge. But, even if he did once forsake the 'despotic book [bouquin]' and engage strenuously in journalism, the articles he wrote for *La Dernière Mode* still have the power to 'set him dreaming long dreams'. For (one might add) they, too, were part of the Book: a linguistic 'transposition' of the material world. And it is as a writer that he describes the relative solitude in which he works. Apart from daily sorties to school – the Lycée Condorcet, the Lycée Janson de Sailly in Passy to which he was inconveniently posted in October 1884, the nearby Collège Rollin to which he had just been mercifully transferred – 'I wander little, preferring above all, in an apartment defended by my family, this sojourn among a few old, cherished pieces of furniture, and the sheet of paper that is often blank.' But it is not a friendless solitude: his 'great friendships' have been with Villiers, Mendès and Manet, and now, of course, thanks to the interest generated by *Les Poètes maudits*, 'my Tuesdays' – 'long empty' – are attended by young poets who think he has influenced them 'when there has simply been a meeting of minds': 'I was ten years ahead' (*oc*, I. 790). He may 'wander' little, therefore, but the world now beats a path to his door.

Finally this is the innovative and authentic writer who had hated Verlaine resurrecting old clichés about 'Mallarmé the mad poet' in *Les Poètes maudits*. 'Here you have my life stripped of anecdotes, unlike those for so long rehashed by the major newspapers, where I have always had the reputation of being very strange.' Instead we have a 'normal' family man who enjoys ballet and organ-music – 'my two almost contradictory passions in art' – and his holidays beside forest and river: 'I honour the river, which allows entire days to be swallowed up in its waters without leaving any impression of their having been wasted nor any shadow of remorse.'

Verlaine respected the content of this letter, including much of it in his article (eventually published in February 1886), and often verbatim. By way of unpublished material he included a new prose poem, 'La Gloire', celebrating the 'glorious' sunsets at Fontainebleau in a language militantly at odds with that of the tourist brochure, and a version of what would later become the sonnet 'Victorieuse-ment fui le suicide beau . . .' (Victoriously fled the fine suicide . . .), itself an erotic account of the solar drama and probably inspired by Méry Laurent.

Gradually, therefore, Mallarmé was emerging into the light, both as the former 'Parnassian' and now also in his latest textual manfestations. Gradually his Tuesdays did indeed become the focus of a whole new generation of poets: not only Kahn and Laforgue, but those who would soon call them themselves 'Symbolists' – notably the Greek-born poet and protégé of Verlaine, Jean Moréas, who unveiled his Symbolist 'manifesto' in *Le Figaro* the following year. Another was René Ghil, who had just published his first collection of verse and would advertise his Symbolist credentials twelve months later in his *Traité du verbe* (Treatise on the Word), for which – despite his distaste for its self-regarding and pretentious author – Mallarmé wrote the preface. The most accomplished of these young poets in Mallarmé's eyes was Henri de Régnier, whose first collection appeared now. American-born François Vielé-Griffin had also just produced his first collection, while Stuart Merrill, the son of an American diplomat in Paris and an enthusiastic reader of Walt Whitman, would publish his in 1887. Like Ghil he had been a pupil of Mallarmé's at the prestigious Lycée Condorcet, and perhaps it was the school connection that led them and others to view Mallarmé as the Master to their Disciple. But, as his letter to Verlaine makes clear, Mallarmé himself was keen to reject this idea – partly out of modesty but more importantly out of a sense that they had not quite understood (no more than Verlaine had) what he was really up to as a poet.

This was evident from the incomprehension that had greeted one of his longest and most accomplished poems, 'Prose (pour des Esseintes)', on its publication in the *Revue indépendante* in January 1885. Ostensibly this poem is a tribute to the hero of *À rebours*, the novel published by Huysmans in May 1884. Jean de Floressas des Esseintes, an aristocrat and aesthete, is a man of exquisite taste, given to studding the shell of his tortoise with precious stones, and his literary preferences, detailed at length, extend particularly and above all to the work of Mallarmé, especially his prose poems. The myth of the élitist, ivory-tower Mallarmé begins here (in chapter Fourteen): '[Des Esseintes] liked the works of this poet who, in an age of lucre and universal suffrage, lived apart from the world of letters, sheltered from the surrounding stupidity by his disdain, taking contented pleasure far removed from the world in the surprises afforded by the intellect and the visions of his own brain.' Nonsense, of course. Huysmans was exaggerating and maybe even (as is suggested by a letter he wrote to Zola) mocking this Tuesday magus. Mallarmé for his part, ever supremely courteous, thanked him by letter and decided to return the dubious compliment by dedicating a poem to the novel's no less dubious hero.

An early draft of 'Prose (pour des Esseintes)' exists, dating back to the early 1870s, and it is plausible to infer from the finished work that its origins lay in Mallarmé's continuing thoughts about the creative tension between the spoken and the written. This tension is a central issue in the *Notes sur le langage* (written about that time), and is reflected in 'Prose' in the dialectic of oral and scriptural methods of 'remembering' or recording language. It is likely that, when *À rebours* appeared, Mallarmé already had a substantially complete version of the poem to hand. Fortuitous connections between some aspects of the novel (lilies, plainchant, Des Esseintes's preference for Mallarmé's prose poetry) made the parenthetical dedication apt, while the text itself is a brilliant example of Mallarméan art that has nothing to do with Huysmans and his mockery.

Consisting of fourteen octosyllabic quatrains in crossed rhyme the poem blends apparent narrative with a purely symbolic logic, evoking an island on which 'the family of the Iridiceae' bloom. The apparently perverse title 'Prose' means not only prose but a 'prosa', a Latin hymn sung during the Mass. More especially, a 'prosa' is the medieval form of octosyllabic plainchant in crossed rhyme that was the source of the convention in French poetry – until this very moment – whereby rhyme was obligatory in verse. As Mallarmé knew, the younger generation, inspired by Verlaine's experiments, was about to launch *vers libre*, in which consistent rhyme and metrical regularity are discarded. With his conception of the *Idée* as a quasi-musical system of 'rhythm between relationships', and having long concurred with Banville's celebrated view that rhyme is the 'flower' of French poetry, Mallarmé was here proclaiming – in practice and by historical allusion – his own abiding faith in the principle of homophony as the cornerstone of the poetic edifice.

The poem represents a virtuoso display of rhyming, both terminal and internal, and the climactic eighth quatrain prompts a reflexive or 'self-allegorical' reading:

Gloire du long désir, Idées
Tout en moi s'exaltait de voir
La famille des iridées
Surgir à ce nouveau devoir, [. . .]

Literally: 'Glory of the long desire, Ideas / everything in me thrilled to see / the family of Iridaceae / rise up to this new duty'. Less literally, the poem here presents punning rhymes as evidence of the power of language to create its own myths, its own 'Idées': the almost anagrammatic coupling of 'désir' and 'Idées' has provided the linguistic seed for a family of symbolic flowers. Similarly, the poem begins with the word 'Hyperbole!', which sets in train a double sequence: the hyperbolic (polysemic, homophonically rich) string of words that follows, and a hyperbola that suggests both the passage of the sun across the sky and the form of a rainbow, its seven colours evoked by the seven quatrains in each half of the poem's simulation of a triumphal arch. Further allusions – to the iris as flower, to the goddess Iris (associated with rainbows), and to the iris of the eye – complement the central focus on the *Idée*: a visual and mental pattern wrought from the chaos intimated by the word 'dé [die/dice]' contained in both 'désir' and 'Idées'. The poem itself thereby (and for many other linguistic reasons within the text) comes to represent the tantalizingly brief triumph of the ordered over the random.

In its evocation of the passage of the sun across the daytime sky 'Prose' recalls the untitled poem that Mallarmé had written the previous year on the fan that he gave to Geneviève, perhaps for her nineteenth birthday. This fan (conserved today at Valvins) consists of white paper, edged with gold and held by sixteen blades of mother-of-pearl. The poem, five octosyllabic quatrains in crossed rhyme, is written in red ink, with the first letter in each line and the final full stop in each stanza written in gold. Many parallels are established between physical object and linguistic text: for example, the first two letters of the poem spell *or* (gold), while the 32 syllables in each quatrain, grouped by rhyme into two units of sixteen, mirror the doubling of folded paper between the sixteen blades. Both ink and words reinforce the suggestive properties of this fan as an emblem of the solar drama: the spread of blades apes the semi-circle of a rising or a setting sun on the 'horizon' (l.8), while the unfurling of the fan would cause its golden edging to simulate the curving passage of the sun across the sky – a passage suggested also in the 'relaying' of the syllable 'or' (as in the 'Sonnet allégorique

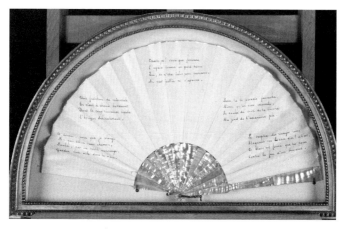

The original version of 'Éventail de Mademoiselle Mallarmé' on the fan that Mallarmé gave Geneviève in 1884.

de lui-même') from the beginning of the poem ('*O rêveuse . . .*') to the end: 'les soirs de l'or' (the evenings of gold), and mention of Geneviève's gold bracelet against which the closed fan will finally be laid.

Like 'Prose' therefore, this poem (eventually entitled 'Autre éventail' [Another fan]) is simultaneously a visual and an aural experience. Like an opera, perhaps. Among the new *mardistes* was Édouard Dujardin, a wealthy young writer and Wagner enthusiast who was then (in 1885) setting up the *Revue wagnérienne* in collaboration with Teodor de Wyzewa. Wagner had died in February 1883, and the two men were eager to promote his music and his theories about the 'total work of art' in a France where memories of the Franco-Prussian war were nevertheless still fresh. On Good Friday Dujardin invited Huysmans and Mallarmé as his guests to a performance of Wagner's music, part of the Lamoureux series of concerts which Mallarmé would henceforth regularly attend. Dujardin then asked both writers to contribute to his new review. Mallarmé's health had again been poor, and was now further undermined by an acute attack of his habitual insomnia. But he had secured three months' sick leave, on full pay, and he accepted.

The result was a dense, complex article, entitled 'Richard Wagner. Rêverie d'un poëte français', which appeared in August. Here, for the first time, Mallarmé produced a type of prose writing – 'half article, half prose poem', as he told Dujardin (*Corr.*, II. 290) – that he would later describe as a 'poëme critique' (in the 'Bibliographie' to his 1897 collection of prose writings, *Divagations*). If a poem could offer a display of language shaping itself into the *Idée*, so too could prose: here, in a form of writing where the argument (the 'critique') is couched in language that exhibits in practice an optimal poetic process against the background of which that 'critique' – in this case of Wagner, later of contemporary theatre and a variety of social institutions – is presented. Just as the poem entitled 'Prose' married narrative with a symbolic logic dictated by the words themselves, so here what purports to be 'prose' (from the Latin *prorsus*, meaning 'straightforward', 'in a direct line') is disrupted in its plain linearity by lexical ambiguity, sinuous syntax, wrong-footing punctuation, and the intercalation of blank spaces between quasi-stanzaic paragraphs of widely differing lengths. Like the later 'divagations', this is the 'rêverie' of a man writing in French by the light of a new poetics, a poetics that had simultaneously prompted his return to the genre of the prose poem with the publication of 'Le Nénuphar blanc' (The White Water-Lily) in the August issue of *L'Art et la Mode*.

Seeming to echo jingoistic nationalism in the title's opposition of Wagner and a French poet, Mallarmé in fact transforms this encounter into a face-off between music and poetry: 'Singular challenge that Richard Wagner inflicts on poets whose duty he usurps with the most candid and splendid bravura!' (*oc*, II. 154). For Mallarmé the 'unpoetic' is constituted by the mimetic, the descriptive and the narrative, which all imply the presence of some grounded truth beyond the realm of language, whereas the 'poetic' is an overtly 'fictional' form of discourse that foregrounds the transience and instability of its own patterning of the world. In his view Wagner is to be praised for taking drama back to its roots: away from the contemporary taste for the mimetic illusionism of naturalistic representation and towards its origins in sacred ritual. But he has gone only so far: the 'temple' of Bayreuth is merely halfway up the 'holy mountain' of the Absolute. In retaining narrative and the particularity of specifically Teutonic myth he has failed to avoid, as he had hoped to, the mere 'juxtaposition' of music and literature: the technique of the leitmotif notwithstanding, he has not, as Mallarmé aspires to, employed the very principles of musical relation in his treatment of the non-musical elements of his 'total work of art'. The absence of dance – 'alone capable, by its summary writing, of translating the fleeting and the sudden to the level of the Idea . . . absolutely the true Spectacle of the future' (*oc*, II. 154) – is damning evidence of the Wagnerian reliance on story: 'here, enthroned above the footlights, is Legend' (*oc*, II. 156).

The French poet, for his part, envisages something more persuasively universal and eternal: a 'Fable, entirely virginal and unblemished by every known place, time, and person', one that will appear 'to unveil itself as deriving from the meaning latent in the assembly of all', a Fable 'inscribed on the page of the Heavens and even whose very History is but interpretation, vain, empty interpretation, that is to say, a Poem, the Ode' (*oc*, II. 157). Wagner's operas continue to imply that myths are discrete and the differences between them therefore significant, perhaps dangerously reinforcing a group tendency – and in particular a national tendency – to believe in Wagner as the only 'conductor', the person who can 'conduct' them on 'humanity's completed journey towards *an* Ideal' (*oc*, II. 158; my emphasis). Rather Mallarmé seeks a form of universal myth, displayed not just in one 'sacred' place like Bayreuth but in a 'mental Holy of Holies' where a universal 'crowd' (as opposed to Wagner's *Volk*) can behold 'the Figure that Nothing/No one is' as it mimes the symphonic rhythms of a global human condition:

> Man, then his authentic terrestrial sojourn, exchange a reciprocity of proofs.

> Thus (the) Mystery.

> The City, which gave, for the sacred experience a theatre, imprints on the earth the universal seal. (*oc*, II. 158)

This echoes what Mallarmé had written to Léo d'Orfer the previous year when requested to provide a definition of poetry: 'Poetry is the expression, by human language restored to its essential rhythm, of the mysterious meaning of the aspects of existence: it thereby endows our sojourn with authenticity and constitutes the sole spiritual task' (*Corr.*, II. 266).

It is clear that Mallarmé was now beginning to expound the 'armature' of his Great Work, the theoretical underpinning of his poetic practice. Just as he was starting to publish a number of his most recent poems, so too he was complementing these 'finished fragments' with increasingly elaborate glimpses of the thinking that lay behind them. In September Dujardin pressed Mallarmé for a further contribution, this time a sonnet in 'homage' to Wagner. The poet was reluctant to spend more time away from his own 'total work of art', being busy

> drafting the Drama, as I see it in my dream, for the best way to describe something is to show it in its finished form. I am working on a first version, which will be the terrible task of my few poor minutes of freedom this winter. . . . At this critical moment in my life (when I must shine forth once and for all)

my thoughts are far from any sort of collaboration, even with the tempting [journals] that you mention. (*Corr.*, II. 294)

As he put it to Maurice Barrès the same day, 'the only drama worth writing . . . is that of Man and the Idea' (*Corr.*, XI. 35). But he duly produced his 'Hommage', a Petrarchan sonnet in alexandrines, in which an overt eulogy of 'the god Richard Wagner' is subtly undermined by allusion to the idolatrous worship of the Golden Calf and the veiled implication that the sybilline silences of Mallarméan verse are more authentic than the noisy trumpets and personality cult of Bayreuth and its 'Man-Magus' (*homme-mage*).

Ever resourceful, and profiting from Mallarmé's ongoing pre-occupation with drama, Dujardin invited him to contribute a series of articles on contemporary theatre to his latest new review, the *Revue indépendante*, which he had co-founded with another *mardiste*, Félix Fénéon. Despite – or perhaps because of – the demands of his own 'Drama', Mallarmé accepted, and the series – entitled 'Notes sur le théâtre' and later *Crayonné au théâtre* (Pencilled in the Theatre) when they were revised and published in *Divagations* – appeared from November 1886 to July 1887. These 'Notes sur le théâtre' covered a wide range of contemporary theatre: a performance of *Hamlet* with the leading actor Mounet-Sully in the title role; Paul Margueritte's *Pierrot assassin de sa femme*; two ballets; some Realist and Naturalist plays, including dramatizations of novels by Zola and Daudet; melodrama; Wagner; the neo-classical theatre of François Ponsard; and Banville's verse drama, *Le Forgeron*. In revising them for *Divagations* Mallarmé added two later articles that he published in the *National Observer* in London in 1893: one on the American dancer Loïe Fuller, another star of the Folies-Bergère, and one on Dujardin's attempt at Wagnerian effects in his trilogy in free verse, *La Légende d'Antonia*.

The thrust of these articles, both in the 1886–7 version and in *Crayonné au théâtre*, is that of the article on Wagner: against mimeticism and towards an 'idealized' form of spectacle in which the *Idée* will be figured in such a way as to satisfy the spiritual hunger of the 'crowd'. Art is not about holding up a mirror to the contemporary bourgeoisie, placating it with a comforting, untroubled representation of its banal everyday activities. In some theatres, Mallarmé writes, it is as though part of the audience had gone up onto the stage and the rest had gone to sit in the stalls: each group dressed and behaving like the other. Art should be at once more disturbing and more satisfying than this, should create a sense of tension as the 'Figure that Nothing / No One is' displays itself in such a way as to mimic and foreground the unconscious existential uncertainties besetting us all. The solar drama – 'the play written on the folio of the sky' – requires to be acted out in the most figurative and least representational manner possible. And in both its original and revised versions this quasi-orchestral suite of articles itself enacts the solar drama, moving from the sunset evoked at the outset (at the beginning of the article on *Hamlet*), through the benighted inadequacy of fashionable mimetic theatre, to the final apotheosis and 'resurrection' represented by Banville's *Le Forgeron* in the article entitled 'Solennités' ('Solemnities', with its potential etymology of 'sun years').

For Mallarmé the theatre is, ideally, a place where human beings join together in undergoing a 'solemn' ritual of cosmic understanding: 'the stage is the evident foyer/hearth/focal point [in French, 'foyer'] of pleasures taken in common, also and all well reflected, the majestic opening onto the mystery whose grandeur it is our purpose in this world to envisage' (*oc*, II. 181). The theatre is 'of superior essence/by its essence superior' (*oc*, II. 179) and able to compensate its audiences for the inadequate, ideologically divisive manner in which the 'City' organises itself: 'the citizen who grasps this idea [thereby] founds the right to claim [such theatre] from the State, as compensation for this social reduction' (*oc*, II. 181).

This is why, for Mallarmé, *Hamlet* is '*the* play . . . *par excellence*': 'for there is no other subject, mark my words: the antagonism between man's dream and the fateful circumstances meted out to his existence by misfortune'. With the minimum of interference from the particularities of place, time, and plot, Hamlet's dilemma is our dilemma – to be caught 'between': between childhood and adulthood, sanity and madness, doing and not doing, life and death. He is the 'latent lord who cannot become', a 'juvenile ghost of us all, partaking thus of myth' (*oc*, ii. 167). Increasingly for Mallarmé – although he had already intimated this in 'Un spectacle interrompu' – the purpose of art is to hold us in suspense: not the foolish suspense of the melodrama, so glibly resolvable, but a suspense that promises a meaning beyond the suspense, a prolonged wondering that opens onto 'Mystery'. The 'fury against the formless' (*oc*, i. 516) prompted by the death of Anatole is to be calmed by the all-embracing 'relations' of the *Idée*, by the 'ministry of the Poet' (*oc*, ii. 203).

As to the poet's art, Mallarmé had just defined this in his short Foreword to Ghil's *Traité du verbe*, which he later incorporated as the final six paragraphs of 'Crise de vers' in *Divagations* (*oc*, ii. 212–13). There are two sorts of language: 'unpolished or immediate', and 'essential'. The former, a kind of 'universal reportage', may suffice 'to narrate, to teach, even to describe', and resembles a currency in everyday use. The other is a way of 'transposing a fact of nature into its vibratory near-disappearance' and of purifying it of all 'proximate and concrete' reference to the world so that 'the pure notion' underlying the 'fact of nature' may emerge:

> I say: a flower! and, out of the oblivion to which my voice relegates every contour [of the flower], musically there arises, as something other than the known calixes upon it, as idea – itself and suave – what is absent from all bouquets.

One thing the word 'flower' is not is a bunch of daffodils; rather it is a linguistic unit. In French 'fleur' homophonically contains both 'l'heure' (the hour) and 'leurre' (trap) – with which, of course, it could rhyme. The 'musical' (i.e. relational) idea that arises might comprise temporality and unreliability, thus linguistically grounding the flower's traditional role as a symbol of seductive but transient beauty.

Mallarmé does not himself make the possibilities of 'fleur' explicit in this way, but instead summarizes:

> Rather than being a form of straightforward hard cash representing something, which is how the crowd treats it, saying something – which first and foremost is dream and song – recovers in the Poet, by the constitutive necessity of an art consecrated to fictions, its virtuality.

When we use a word – and the implication here is that we could all be poets – we need to 'dream' of all its possible properties and meanings and then forge connections between them in the 'musical relationships' of song (itself the etymological sense of the 'Ode' to which Mallarmé refers in his letter to Verlaine and his essay on Wagner). If a 'poem', like a 'fiction', is a 'making', a 'fabrication', then all speech acts are potentially poems, which is why in fact all of us – the crowd – are engaged in one and the same activity. The 'ministry' of the poet, at once religious and political, is to guide the people towards that realization. The line of verse – 'which from several vocables remakes a word and renders it total, new, foreign to the language' – is thus a form of 'isolation': of 'isolating' or separating out the unique contingent features of a word but also 'insulating' it (like the 'insula' or island in 'Prose') against the wear and tear of habitual use, of the unthinking association of the *sound* of 'fleur' with those daffodils. The result is, Mallarmé concludes, that the word itself now surprises you, as though you had never heard it before; and that the object to which it conventionally refers 'is bathed in a new atmosphere'. Poetry allows us to breathe the oxygen of a new world and to perceive new flowers.

Félicien Rops's 'La Grande Lyre', the frontispiece for the 1887 *Revue indépendante* edition of Mallarmé's *Poésies*.

So does Mallarmé's first collection of *Poésies*, published in 1887. Dujardin encouraged Mallarmé to think of publishing a collection of his verse, a kind of retrospective in print. Accordingly the reluctant self-publicist revisited his files, adjusted and revised, and then produced fair copies of his selected poems, each in his own elegant handwriting. The collection comprised 35 poems, of which three were published here for the first time: 'Le Pitre châtié' (The Clown Chastised) and the final versions of 'Victorieusement fui le suicide beau . . .' and 'Ses purs ongles très haut dédiant leurs onyx . . .'. These were then reproduced by the new process of photolithography and published in October under the imprint of the *Revue indépendante*, nine 'cahiers' grouped together as a book with a frontispiece by the Belgian printmaker Félicien Rops.

It was a landmark of sorts, but the Great Work remained. As Mallarmé had written one year earlier to another *mardiste*, the Italian critic Vittorio Pica:

> I believe that Literature, by going back to its source which is [both] Art and Science, will furnish us with a Theatre in which the performances will be the true cult of the modern age; a Book, an explanation of man, sufficient unto our finest dreams. I believe the whole thing to be written in nature, so that only those who have an interest in not seeing can shut their eyes to it. This work exists, everybody has attempted it without realizing that they were doing so; there is not one single genius or fairground barker who has uttered a word and not uncovered some aspect of it without realizing the fact. To demonstrate this and to raise one corner of the veil from what such a poem can be, this is, within my isolation, at once my torture and my pleasure . . . (*Corr.*, III. 73).

There would still be plenty to talk about on Tuesdays.

6

Toasts

Verlaine and Dujardin had together served to bring the *Poésies* into the light, and Mallarmé felt the weight of his new celebrity among the *mardistes*. He himself, of course, had helped to foster their great expectations, but this did not prevent him from complaining to Dujardin:

> Out of kind friendship you have placed on my somewhat ageing shoulders the magnificent burden of a destiny that I may have dreamt of for someone, if not myself; life – deteriorating health (still the same old problem at night) and growing servitude (I shall not return to the Lycée Condorcet) – now presents me with the prospect of disappointment. (*Corr.*, III. 53)

The insomnia and consequent eyestrain was so bad that his doctor ordered him to wear a blindfold – 'a real one this time' (*Corr.*, III. 78) – for nearly a month and not write a single word. It must have reminded Mallarmé of his days of nervous illness in Tournon when he had had to dictate his letters to Marie.

The celebrity grew as Mallarmé's reputation began to spread beyond France and England, to Italy (with Vittorio Pica), Germany (thanks to Stefan George, also a *mardiste*), and Belgium, where a literary golden age was dawning. The poet Émile Verhaeren, whom Huysmans had brought along to a *mardi* and whom Mallarmé came to consider as the most original and accomplished poet among his compatriots, had brought Mallarmé's *Poésies* to the attention of the Belgian public in a perceptive review. At the same time a very slim volume of Mallarmé's work (in sixteen duodecimo pages), the *Album de vers et de prose*, was published in Brussels in December.

Mallarmé's former scruples about 'albums' and random selections had clearly been set to one side – 'I am liquidating my past', as he told Verhaeren (*Corr.*, III. 162) – and he envisaged another 'album': a prose counterpart to the *Poésies*. It would bring together his prose poems, his preface to *Vathek*, and his article on Wagner. Following the republication in March 1887 of *L'Après-midi d'vn favn – Églogve* (now with Latinized, quasi-Virgilian title and still with Manet's illustrations), he was keen to continue this practice of publishing his work in fine-art editions. Berthe Morisot and her husband Eugène Manet (the late painter's brother) had been staying near Valvins that summer, and he hoped on the basis of their growing friendship that she might illustrate his prose poem 'Le Nénuphar blanc'. The so-called 'Banquet Years' were now underway, and ever since the banquet in January 1885 marking the Manet retrospective Mallarmé had been attending the regular dinners held by the Impressionists. (Morisot's were on Thursdays.) So he approached Renoir (for 'Le Phénomène futur'), Monet (for 'La Gloire'), and Degas to see if they also would contribute to his proposed volume, to be entitled *Le Tiroir de laque* (The Lacquered Drawer). Inspired by the current taste for Japanese art, Mallarmé intended that each page of text, duly illustrated, would thus resemble the exquisitely decorated drawer of a chest or bureau. In the event the only friend to produce something was Renoir, whose etching of a female nude depicted the 'Woman of Yesteryear' in 'Le Phénomène futur'. Eventually this became the frontispiece of an otherwise unillustrated Belgian anthology of Mallarmé's prose writings, entitled *Pages* and published in Brussels in 1891 by Edmond Deman. The latter, initially suggested by Verhaeren who had been his close friend as a student and was now one of his authors, became Mallarmé's principal publisher for the rest of his life, not just a man of commerce but a keen bibliophile, at once sympathetic to his author's high standards based on precise aesthetic criteria and heroically tolerant of his vacillations about style and font.

Mallarmé's contacts with the world of painting proliferated and deepened during these years. Morisot, Monet, Renoir and Degas were regular dinner companions, as were Gustave Caillebotte, Pierre Puvis de Chavannes and Mary Cassatt, the American artist now resident in Paris whom Mallarmé also approached for his *Tiroir de laque*. In the American-born London resident James McNeill Whistler he found another soulmate: an artist of very similar outlook and who seemed to him to be the living embodiment of his fellow American, Edgar Allan Poe.

With the aid of the Franco-American, Francis Vielé-Griffin, Mallarmé translated Whistler's *Ten O'Clock Lecture* (1885), a defence of the autonomy of art and the artist against those who would annex it in the name of education, public morality or dilettante aestheticism. It was published in the *Revue indépendante* in May 1888. In November 1890 Mallarmé provided Whistler with a witty sonnet in octosyllabic metre for the painter's new (and shortlived) journal, *The Whirlwind*, which described itself as 'a lively and eccentric newspaper'. Written in playful homage to Whistler and eventually entitled 'Billet', the poem provides the eponymous ticket to a linguistic display that simulates the 'whirlwind' of a ballerina's pirouette: it performs a syntactic balancing act, having no main verb and being yet full of motion, like a circular dance going nowhere, and it uses the closing couplet required by the Shakespearean form of the sonnet to end, on its points, with the flourish of a virtuoso rhyme on 'Whistler'. 'Superb and dandy' was Whistler's delighted response. He was even more delighted the following year when Mallarmé played a key role in persuading the French state to purchase his *Arrangement in Gray and Black*:

James McNeill Whistler's lithograph portrait of Mallarmé for use as the frontis-piece of *Vers et Prose* (1892), here with Whistler's dedication 'To my Mallarmé'. Mallarmé thought this portrait 'a marvel' and the only one truly to capture him: 'I'm giving myself a smile'.

Portrait of the Artist's Mother. The price may have been slightly disappointing, but the accompanying appointment as Chevalier in the Legion of Honour was not. Thus decorated, Whistler moved to Paris permanently.

Mallarmé's relations with painters varied. Sometimes they painted or drew him: not only Manet, but Gauguin (1891), Whistler (1892, in Mallarmé's preferred likeness of himself), Renoir (1892, which he hated), Félix Vallotton (1895), Edvard Munch (1897). Occasionally they simply gave him a painting, as Morisot did in 1893 (a small oil depicting his boat at Valvins), and as Monet did when Mallarmé visited Giverny with Morisot in 1890 and himself chose *Le Train à Jeufosse* as his gift. His living-room in the rue de Rome became an Impressionist art gallery in miniature. He also wrote poems to accompany their work, as in the case of Jean-François Raffaëlli, a friend of the Impressionists but himself a largely Realist painter and printmaker who was now specializing in street scenes. Together with other writers (Zola, Maupassant, Huysmans, Daudet et al.) Mallarmé collaborated on a series entitled *Les Types de Paris* (1889), providing two sonnets about a cobbler and a lavender-seller and five quatrains on other 'low-born' representatives of the urban scene. The playful contrivance and humorous self-deprecation of these 'Chansons bas' – not 'low songs' but 'songs sung low' – display a poet every bit as ready to take poetry into the street as the artist was to take his sketch-pad. And Mallarme's first such intermedia collaboration, with Manet on *L'Après-midi d'un faune* and then on Poe's 'Raven', now reached its culmination in 1888 when Deman published his translation, *Les Poèmes d'Edgar Poe*, complete with Manet's pen and ink portrait of Poe and two decorative tail-pieces.

The publication of the *Poésies*, the *Album de vers et de prose*, and the Poe volume all helped Mallarmé to 'liquidate his past', and from this point on it seems indeed as though he had been set free from a heavy burden and now felt able to experiment in all directions. The Petrarchan sonnet, for example, had been his preferred verse form, but he now experimented with the Shakespearean form, marrying its rhyme scheme (abab cdcd efef gg) with the stanzaic divisions of the Petrarchan sonnet into

quatrains and tercets in some sixteen sonnets written before his
death. The first such, 'La chevelure vol d'une flamme . . .' (The hair,
flight of a flame . . .), was published as part of a new prose poem,
'La Déclaration foraine' (Fairground Declaration), in *L'Art et la
Mode* in August 1887. The prose poem itself tells a story of the
poet accompanying a lady on an afternoon carriage ride. They
stop to walk through a fairground, encountered by chance, and
when the lady unexpectedly steps up to display herself, elegantly
clad, in an empty fairground booth, the poet feels obliged to reward
the resultant crowd by reciting his sonnet. The sonnet itself is a
variation on the old conceit whereby the poet celebrates his companion's beauty by lamenting his own inadequacy to capture it
in verse, while the whole prose poem may be read as a reflexive
allegory of this very attempt to achieve beauty through the
'downmarket' or fairground media of the prose poem and the
Shakespearean sonnet.

   The latter had been and still was regarded as irregular and
unworthy within the French prosodic tradition, and Mallarmé was
virtually its only exponent. Plainly he was attempting, in response
to the advent of *vers libre*, to take French poetry in new directions
but without sacrificing the prosodic order that he had always
regarded as indispensable to the poetic 'fabrication' of the *Idée*. For
similar reasons he now experimented with different line lengths,
heeding Verlaine's innovative preference for the imparisyllabic line
and producing several sonnets in heptasyllabic metre. At the same
time he began to experiment with the suppression of punctuation
in his poems, believing that this was restrictive and even otiose in
the fashioning of multiple syntactic patterns otherwise governed
and orchestrated by metrical and stanzaic structure. His first such
experiment – the octosyllabic sonnet 'M'introduire dans ton histoire
. . .' (To introduce myself into your story . . .) – had appeared in
Léo d'Orfer's newly-founded *La Vogue* in June 1886. His resolve
had faltered temporarily in the face of the adverse criticism this

provoked, and, as he told Dujardin, he included punctuation in his 'Triptyque' of sonnets published in the *Revue indépendante* the following January 'because all things considered it's better to have people off our backs' (*Corr.,* III. 75). But subsequently he persisted with the experiment in an increasing number of poems, culminating in the radical, unpunctuated layout of *Un coup de Dés* in 1897.

Mallarmé's sense of liberation and his increasing desire to take on the younger generation with poetic experimentation far bolder than theirs suggests also that he was becoming more and more conscious that the Great Work would never be written, at least not by him. Instead, having always held fire until this work would be complete, he now seemed determined to leave his mark in whatever way he could. Thus, in 1891, he signed a contract with Deman for a collection of his *Poésies*, perhaps now to be called *Vers*, and which would include all his latest work. In the event this volume would be published only after his death, in 1899.

Mallarmé had now also returned to the genre of the prose poem, first with 'Le Nénuphar blanc' in 1886. In this tremulous evocation of a soporific, unaccompanied boating excursion along the Seine, reminiscent of *L'Après-midi d'un faune*, the prose-poet nearly but not quite chances to espy a female neighbour walking in her riverside garden: unmet, 'unhatched', she can remain like the egg-shaped bloom of a water lily replete with the unfurled petals of the might-have-been. A similar passing glimpse, no doubt while visiting Méry Laurent at her house in the Bois de Boulogne, gave rise to 'L'Écclésiastique', a wry, richly suggestive account of a frocked priest rolling voluptuously in the long grass of the Bois in onanistic and hermaphroditically self-sufficient celebration of the advent of spring. First published, discreetly, by Vittoria Pica in the *Gazetta letteraria* in Turin in December 1886, it appeared in the *Revue indépendante* in April 1888. As in 'Le Nénuphar blanc' and 'La Déclaration foraine', the prose poem seems here to serve appropriately as a kind of 'crossover' genre, presenting the banally or humorously quotidian from the perspective of a more lasting symbolic purport: 'remarking events in a light appropriate to dream' (*oc*, I. 420). The journey – a boat trip, a carriage ride, a walk – betokens the random experience of a post-Baudelairean *flâneur*, while the highly intricate use of language bears witness to the transformative work of a poet.

The playfulness that Mallarmé exhibits in these and other prose poems is evident also in the so-called *Vers de circonstance*, or 'occasional verse', that he produced throughout these years and which he, with the help of his daughter (and later her husband), preserved for posterity. The fan-poem that he had given her in 1883 was itself the first major example, to be followed by the fan-sonnets given to Méry Laurent (1890) and then – last and perhaps least – to his wife Marie (1891). Other quatrains appeared on fans offered as presents to female friends, as they did on all manner of gift and object: books, photographs, Easter eggs . . . Through the incorporation of proper names and deft allusion to circumstance or characteristic, whether of the receiver or of the object itself, the material reality of the world is transmuted into a verbal construct of symbolic significance. As his future son-in-law Edmond Bonniot recorded later: 'he had only to spend a few minutes staring at an object for the pure sign to emerge from it. He would say he was reading the object' (*Corr.*, VI. 31, n. 3).

Some of the *galets* that Mallarmé inscribed with verse, and his elegant monogram, during summer holidays at Honfleur in the 1890s.

It was Mallarmé's practice at New Year, for example, to make gifts of *fruits glacés*, or candied fruit. They too, at this key calendular juncture, performed the solar drama. Pieces of sun-like orange or dawn-pink apple, harvested in autumn and dusted with frost-like sugar, would be meltingly resurrected in the vernal warmth of the receiver's mouth as they ate the gift – and spoke the accompanying words that intimated these symbolic associations. When in the mid-1890s, with Marie and Geneviève, Mallarmé spent several summer holidays at Honfleur at the home of Marguerite Ponsot (mother of a favourite pupil, Willy, and of Geneviève's close friend Éva), the poet would gather flat stones (*galets*) from the beach and 'decorate' them with couplets in honour of his wife and daughter, his hostess, her children, or other friends. A couplet . . . sufficient for one rhyme, and thus for one emblematically clinched conceit manifesting the power of poetry to quell the 'fury of the formless' and (through Geneviève's subsequent transcription) to save the ephemeral for eternity: for example, 'With this one, Joseph, whom I teach, / you'll play ducks and drakes upon the beach', or 'For Françoise who serves at table / so many dishes, so de-lect-able' (*oc*, i. 347, 349).

From this period onwards Mallarmé was also in the habit of couching the addresses of his friends in the form of rhyming quatrains that contained the salient information and which, he claimed, did not defeat a single French postman. Just for fun he sent one to himself. The first such 'quatrain-adresse' dates from 1885: its addressee, Verlaine, replied that 'it just goes to show that with rich rhyme . . . you can do anything' (*oc*, i. 1248). Whistler learnt of the practice in February 1892 and tried to interest London publishing houses in the project. When it seemed as though he had succeeded, Mallarmé prepared a manuscript of some 89 addresses, entitling them *Récréations postales*, but this project came to nought. In Chicago, however, Harrison G. Rhodes, a recent *mardiste* and editor of the newly founded avant-garde review *The Chap Book*, published 27 of them under the new title of *Les Loisirs de la poste* (Postal Pastimes) on 15 December 1894. Pride of place in both collections went to Whistler and his new wife, Trixie Godwin, widow of the E. W. Godwin who had designed Whistler's London residence, 'The White House', in Chelsea:

Leur rire avec la même gamme
Sonnera si tu te rendis
Chez Monsieur Whistler et Madame,
Rue antique du Bac 110.

'Their laughter with the same [notes on the] scale / will sound if you go / to Monsieur Whistler and Madame, / ancient rue du Bac [old Ferry Street] 110.

The Mallarmé who emerges from these *Vers de circonstance* (which were eventually published in their entirety in 1920 by Geneviève Mallarmé and her husband) is the Mallarmé for whom Tuesday evening was now almost the *only* evening on which he was actually at home, a gregarious Mallarmé with many friends, admirers and acquaintances who was sometimes at the theatre and almost always at the Sunday concerts of Lamoureux or Colonne, who was constantly dining with Méry Laurent (often after these concerts) or at other people's houses (sometimes accompanied by Geneviève), or else at restaurants where writers and artists now regularly held their 'banquets'.

This is also the Mallarmé who got things done, making sure, for example, that not only a Whistler but a Renoir were bought by the French state. In the summer of 1889, with Paris agog at the Universal Exhibition and other celebrations being held to celebrate the centenary of the Revolution (and marvelling at the newly erected Eiffel Tower, the tallest building in the world), Mallarmé learnt that his elusive friend Villiers – who had been ill for some time – was in fact dying of stomach cancer. Villiers lived in reduced circumstances with his illiterate common-law wife Marie Brégeras (née Dantine) and their son Victor. Mallarmé, Huysmans and Méry Laurent formed an informal support group, and it fell to Mallarmé to try and persuade his friend to marry Marie in order to legitimate their son and thus entitle him to state assistance as a minor. The Breton aristocrat jibbed at first, but four days before his death (on 19 August) he acquiesced. Méry Laurent, unable to be present, paid for Marie's wedding ring and a celebratory bottle of Veuve Cliquot. At the funeral (again in her absence) Méry's magnificent wreath of lilies took pride of place beside a simple crown of laurels (to honour a poet), Mallarmé having removed one lily to place it in their friend's coffin, itself draped in a black pall decorated with Villiers' coat-of-arms. Mallarmé got Villiers' widow to make over to him (nominally) all the goods and chattels she had just inherited so that they could not be seized as payment for outstanding debts. Villiers had named Huysmans and himself as his literary executor, and together they did what they could to tidy up some unpublished material so that its publication might bring Marie much-needed income and their late friend further acclaim. The completion of Villiers' last play, *Axël*, was their achievement, with its famous line: 'Live? The servants will do that for us.' In the circumstances it took on a new meaning.

At the same time Mallarmé responded to the request of his Belgian writer-friends to visit and lecture in Belgium, now not on his own behalf but to present a memorial tribute to Villiers. The latter had himself undertaken a lecture tour of Belgium in February–March 1888, staying with Deman and his wife in Brussels for part of the time, and had been invited back. Mallarmé would go in his stead as the surviving spokesman for the literary ideal they shared. The idea of a lecture, and of giving readings from Villiers' work, happened to chime with his own current preoccupations. In

January 1888 Mallarmé had told Verhaeren of a 'great project': 'it is to present myself in public, around October . . . and to juggle with the content of a book' (*Corr.*, III. 162). On 1 November he mentioned to Berthe Morisot that he was 'working hard, still on the *Readings, four* of which are for next year' (*Corr.*, III. 275). Three weeks later he wrote to Deman: 'I am advancing in the perpetration of my great mysterious project of the Readings' (*oc*, I. 802). Some of the notes that survived after his death suggest that he may be referring here to a proposed 'ceremony of the Book', with himself as 'operator' conducting a series of readings (of his own work) by a fixed number of participants.

Accordingly Mallarmé travelled to Belgium: it had been intended that Geneviève would accompany him, but she was prevented by a bout of 'flu. There, from 10–19 February 1890, he gave his lecture in a series of cities – Brussels, Antwerp, Ghent, Liège, Brussels again and Bruges – and met with a mixture of appreciation from the happy few and angry ridicule from the baffled many. His first performance lasted two and a half hours, and so he reduced it to nearer an hour by truncating or omitting the long quotations from Villiers' own work and, presumably, by pruning his own text. This literary memorial, published soon afterwards, perhaps constitutes Mallarmé's prose masterpiece. It is especially difficult of access and would certainly have been very difficult to follow as a live lecture, but it constitutes a deeply thought-out and densely – indeed concisely! – expressed tribute both to Villiers and through him (as the epitome of the 'authentic writer') to literature.

The lecture begins with a discussion of what it means to 'write': this 'ancient and very vague but jealous practice, the sense of which lies in the mystery of the heart'. It proceeds subsequently to give an ambitious, all-encompassing statement about what the 'sense' of writing might be, which can be translated as follows (with some elucidation and indications of the original French in square brackets):

For as much as something exists (or so we hear [i.e. through language]), and for as much especially as the human species [*soi spécialement*] exists in the reflection of scattered divinity, then writing – in itself an absurd, senseless game [since there is no transcendental authority for it, no divine text to be deciphered] – is the arrogation by human beings, in virtue of a doubt – the drop of ink related to the sublime night -, of some duty to recreate everything, with reminiscences [i.e. by 're-minding' it in language], in order to aver that human beings are happy / indeed where they are supposed to be [also, are happy / indeed in this place where they are obliged to be: in French, *on est bien là où l'on doit être*] (for – please allow me to express this apprehension – an uncertainty persists). One by one, each of our sources of pride, call them up, in their anteriority and see. Otherwise, if that were not it, a summoning of the world to equate its haunting to some rich postulates – enciphered, as its law, on the paper pale at [or 'pale paper of '] so much audacity – I believe, truly, that there would be dupery, almost to the point of suicide. (*OC*, II. 23)

In other words, the act of writing summons the contingent universe (in all its shadowy elusiveness) to conform to the 'musical' patterns that have been wrought by the intellect and language-use of the writer. The writer's task is to go back to first principles, to re-examine the supposed sum of human knowledge, to question all our fond, proud assumptions. The written text will postulate new and richly suggestive connections or relationships within the universe and boldly set them down on paper, as signs or ciphers having the authority of the law. Any other response to the contingency of a godless universe would be tantamount to bad faith or even suicide. Suicide? Partly because this would, as Albert Camus later suggested in *The Myth of Sisyphus*, represent a form of intellectual suicide, but more particularly because for Mallarmé 'suicide' means the killing of the *soi*, the French term meaning 'oneself' or 'itself' that he uses as shorthand at the beginning of this passage and elsewhere for the fundamentals of our shared humanity.

In the remainder of the lecture, divided into four parts like the solar year, Mallarmé militantly avoids any anecdotal, narrative biography but rather transforms Villiers into a living and now deceased embodiment of the very act of writing, 'a pure hero of letters' (*oc*, II. 49). Alluding obliquely nevertheless to his ancestry, his love of music, his noctambulism, his charismatic presence at the *mardis*, his habit of turning up at cafés and reciting from the manuscripts that he would produce like a magician out of his capacious coat-pockets, he 'transfigures' him into a symbol of the combined oral and scriptural properties of a literary text. He *is* the Book – that Book which Villiers had himself envisaged early in his career (in *Isis*) but never completed, the Book that Mallarmé, too, had tried under his influence to write and, most probably, never would. Unless, of course, in this very lecture he were writing it here and now . . . 'an executed fragment' to demonstrate the power and authenticity of the dream he had shared with his eccentric friend.

Both on the page and in its recitation, not least when Mallarmé reprised his performance for some 30 writers and artists at Berthe Morisot's studio on his return, this lecture is itself a mixture of theatrical event (complete with stage directions: 'the speaker sits', 'the speaker rises') and religious service. For Mallarmé, of course, there was no fundamental difference between these: each is, potentially, a symbolic enactment of the solar drama and a public performance of the *Idée*. Moreover, in giving the lecture Mallarmé similarly divests himself of his own subjective particularity and becomes a 'pure hero of letters', another 'torch-bearer' handing on the golden flame of the literary from Villiers to the writers and poets of Belgium. And this performance of the literary, through a reflexive blend of theory and illustrative practice, was how Mallarmé became in public what he had been for so long in the half-private, half-public domain of his *mardis*: the protagonist of the 'Drama' and 'Mystery' that were at the centre of his plans for the Book. Like Paul Margueritte he was both creator and interpreter of a kind of textual mime, and the many banquets of these 'Banquet Years' allowed him further opportunities to perform.

On 2 February 1891 a dinner was held for 80 people in honour of Jean Moréas, who had just published a new collection of poems, *Le Pélerin passionné* [The Passionate Pilgrim], to great, ephemeral acclaim. Here, in a hotel in the rue Serpente just off the Boulevard Saint-Michel, Mallarmé presided, doubtless pleased in his brief toast not only to honour Moréas but to celebrate the solar drama of an occasion that had united 'a whole auroral youth with some ancestors' (*oc*, II. 685). The 'ancestors' included Banville, Heredia, Sully Prudhomme, Dierx, and Mendès, while – suspended between dawn and dusk – the generation born between 1855 and 1865 was represented by Moréas himself, Paul Adam, a Symbolist novelist who had co-written with Moréas *Les Demoiselles Goubert* (1886), Vielé-Griffin, de Régnier, and others. Among the 'auroral youth' were new talents – and *mardistes* – such as the Belgian-born poets André Fontainas, another pupil of Mallarmé's at the Lycée Condorcet (like Ghil and Merrill) and a loyal *mallarmiste* throughout his life, and Pierre Louÿs, who was about to publish his collection of erotic verse, *Astarte*, in *La Conque*. Louÿs in turn was a close friend of Debussy, who had already set some of Mallarmé's work to music, and also of André Gide, another enthusiastic *mardiste* throughout the 1890s. One notable absentee, however, was Verlaine, who had taken umbrage at being invited so late and in any case took a jaundiced view of what he called 'cymbalism'. Mallarmé honoured him by proposing his own toast with discreet ambiguity 'au nom du cher absent Verlaine', meaning a toast '*to* the name of' as well as '*in* the name of' – a name, indeed, that begins with verse.

Paul Gauguin's 1891 etching of Mallarmé. The bird is an allusion to Mallarmé's translation of Edgar Allan Poe's poem 'The Raven'.

As he presided over this assembly of poets, painters and other artists, Mallarmé was no doubt conscious more than ever of life as an 'interregnum', a passing moment comprised at once of the 'desuetude' and the 'preparatory effervescence' he had described in his 'autobiographical' letter to Verlaine. Generations of writers

Mallarmé in his bedroom at 89 rue de Rome, *c*. 1893. Displayed in the cabinet are Rochegrosse's engraving of 1886 of Théodore Banville (with dog and trademark beret) and a photograph of Baudelaire, two poets of particular importance to Mallarmé's own aesthetic development.

and artists come and go, but the existential condition and the fundamental principles of art remain. The function of the living is to pass on the flame. Cyclicity was again on the menu on 23 March when Mallarmé presided at the banquet held to bid farewell to Paul Gauguin, who had just held a major sale of his paintings and was setting off on his great Polynesian adventure in search of new land-scapes and artistic renewal. 'Gentlemen', Mallarmé proposed in his toast, 'in order to proceed with greatest haste, let us drink to the return of Paul Gauguin; but not without admiring this proud mentality, which, in the blaze of his talent, is exiling him – so that he may reimmerse himself – towards distant lands and towards the self [*soi-même*]' (*oc*, II. 685). Where once Poe had been changed 'into Himself' by eternity, the future would unite the departing solar 'blaze' of Gauguin with that *soi* which is the common denominator of our humanity, and so return him to us.

Eleven days earlier Mallarmé had been interviewed at home by the journalist Jules Huret, writing for *L'Écho de Paris*, who was investigating the direction that literature was now taking, particularly in the wake of the widespread publicity secured by Moréas for the publication of *Le Pélerin passionné*. In the resulting article, which the interviewee approved before publication, Huret describes his interlocutor:

> Medium build, beard greying and shaped to a point, a large, straight nose, long, pointed ears like a satyr's, wide, elongated eyes that shine with extraordinary brilliance, a singular expression of shrewdness tempered by a great air of kindness. When he talks, his words are always accompanied by multiple gestures, full of grace, precision and eloquence: the voice lingers slightly over the ends of words, fading gradually; a powerful charm emanates from the man, in whom one can discern a lasting pride, soaring above everything, the pride of a god or a visionary before whom one must immediately make an inward bow – when one has understood him. (*oc*, II. 697)

In the interview itself Huret records, seemingly verbatim, Mallarmé's views on recent literary trends. The interviewee comments first on the new generation of poets, who have rejected the formal regularity of the Parnassians and espoused *vers libre*. In the irregularity of *vers libre* and in the very broad variety of the uses to which it has been put, Mallarmé sees a reflection of the divided and unstable nature of contemporary society. But he welcomes these experiments. The Parnassians were too explicit, too descriptive and narrative, in their poetry whereas the *verslibristes* are truer, in their musicality and suggestiveness, to the 'poetic ideal'. They allow their readers 'that delicious joy of thinking that they themselves are creating the poem':

To name an object is to suppress three quarters of the enjoy-
ment of the poem, which consists in slowly putting two and two
together: to *suggest* it, that is the dream. It is the perfect use of
this mystery that constitutes the symbol: to evoke an object
little by little in order to display a state of soul [*état d'âme*], or,
conversely, to choose an object and to bring out a state of soul
from it, by a series of decipherments. (*oc*, II. 700; Mallarmé's
emphases).

Poetry is bound to involve 'work' on the part of its reader, and it
may be that some readers are insufficiently intelligent or educated
about literature to understand it. But 'there must always be enigma
in poetry, and it is the purpose of literature – there are no others –
to *evoke* objects' (Mallarmé's emphasis); and by 'evoke' he means
'to call up', not to state or describe but to conjure up, like spirits
from another world.

Mallarmé goes on to deny that he has created the new 'movement'
in literature. 'I abominate schools', he says with feeling, meaning not
only literary schools and doubtless his own place of employment,
but 'everything that is professorial applied to literature, which, on
the contrary, is entirely individual'. And for a poet in a society like
his own, 'which does not permit him a living', this 'individuality' is
a form of provisional but paradoxical isolation: 'I believe that poetry
is made for ceremonial and is the highest pomp and circumstance of
a constituted society that has a place for the glory which people seem
to have lost all notion of.' The poet has to cut himself off and 'sculpt
his own tomb', has to live as though he were 'on strike' against society,
carefully dispensing with 'all the vitiated means' that might compro-
mise him: 'No matter what is offered to him will be inferior to his
conception and his secret work.' In short, this period is one in which
the poet is an 'outlaw' (*oc*, II. 701).

As to the new school of Naturalism, Mallarmé praises Zola for
his 'evocatory art', for his ability to capture life, his depiction of

crowds, his powerful painterly descriptions that allow us all, for example, 'to caress the grain of Nana's skin'. But it is just too pat, too accessible. 'Literature has something more intellectual than that', he contends: 'things exist, we don't need to create them; what we have to do is grasp the relations between them; and it is the threads of these relations that form lines of verse and orchestras' (*oc*, ii. 702). Poetry does 'create' but in a different sense:

> Since poetry consists in *creating*, one must capture states in the human soul, gleams of such absolute purity that, well sung and well presented to the light, they constitute in effect the jewels of man: then there is symbol, then there is creation, and the word 'poetry' now has its meaning: it is, in sum, the only human creation possible. (*oc*, ii. 701; Mallarmé's emphasis)

Often 'état d'âme' is translated as 'mood' or 'feeling', but Mallarmé very specifically has in mind the way in which a particular object or experience, however banal or apparently meaningless, in fact serves a function for a 'state of soul' of which we may be only sub-liminally conscious. Why indeed do we treasure jewels? Why do women wear them? Pretty to look at? Status symbols? For Mallarmé (who writes about them particularly in *La Dernière Mode)* they are like the chandeliers that 'preside' over dramatic spectacles: multi-faceted sources and reflectors of light, twinkling like stars in the night sky – or like illuminating works of art in the existential void. As he told Huret with a chuckle, a woman who wears jewels is no better than a shoplifter if she does not realize the 'hidden meaning' of her accessory, 'which consequently does not belong to her . . .' For she has decked herself out in the solar drama.

In retrospect one can see that the poem written on Geneviève's fan, and on others', is therefore a way of explaining its 'hidden meaning' so that the recipient truly owns it: by virtue of poetic art rather than a mere monetary transaction or even the simple acts of donation and receipt. Thus shall readers of poetry be the only true owners of the world we live in. Or, as Mallarmé wrote to Vielé-Griffin on 7 August 1891: 'The whole mystery is there, to establish secret identicalnesses [*identités*] with a two-by-two that gnaws and rubs away at objects, in the name of a central purity' (*Corr.*, IV. 293). Similarly in Part III of the memorial lecture on Villiers (*OC*, II. 41), Mallarmé compares his own ceremony of the Book with the lady in her drawing-room (and implicitly with Méry at her new villa on the site of Les Talus in the Bois de Boulogne, which he was helping her to decorate and furnish with antiques): she will fail to achieve a satisfactory arrangement of her acquisitions unless she understands their symbolic value. The merest *bibelot* can represent the solar drama, but you have to know that it does.

Mallarmé's ability to wrest symbolic significance from the seemingly trivial and routine was further manifested during the series of banquets inaugurated by *La Plume*, a review recently founded by the poet and novelist Léon Deschamps and which had first appeared on 15 April 1889. Until his premature death ten years later Deschamps would run it as a flagship for the Symbolist movement in the arts, particularly literature and painting. As part of his campaign he inaugurated a tradition of bi-monthly banquets, and on 6 December 1892 it was the turn of Leconte de Lisle to be honoured at the sixth such banquet. Falling ill at the last moment the acknowledged leader of the Parnassians deputed Mallarmé to preside in his stead, and this now practised exponent of banquet etiquette read out part of a letter in which the absentee sends word of his thanks to Zola, Coppée and others for having proposed him for the honour. This 'word', Mallarmé observed before reading it out, 'has thus conserved for our celebratory feast [*fête*] – superb, venerable, dear [*chère*] – the integrity of his Presence' (*OC*, II. 686).

Those listening would have realized that the three adjectives qualified all three nouns (feast, integrity, Presence), and they may even have heard the pun on 'chère' (also a noun, meaning 'food, fare') that praises the meal itself with witty exaggeration as 'superb, venerable'. But they would have 'heard' the capital letter on 'Presence' only if they realized that the author of the 'Sonnet en yx' was turning a banquet into the Eucharist, that 'chère' was also the French 'chair', meaning flesh. In this simplest and most banal of circumstances – a last-minute indisposition – the poet turns celebrant, using words to perform a secular miracle of resurrection in summoning presence from absence. Just as Verlaine, the 'dear absentee', had been brought into the room by words, so too had the author of the *Poèmes antiques*: the man who was to have presided from the 'chaire' (chair, pulpit, throne) was enabled by the magic of language to be present as food and flesh. And Mallarmé concluded: 'I raise this glass [*verre*], in the name of / to the name of Leconte de Lisle, to all, to Poetry, which we follow him in representing.' As he had indicated in his famous letter to Verlaine, all writers – all language-users – are essentially engaged in the same task, the labour of the Book.

Following Mallarmé's toast, Deschamps read out another section of Leconte de Lisle's letter in which the poet himself proposed that Mallarmé should succeed him in the chair at the next banquet, on 9 February 1893. The chain would be unbroken. At that banquet Mallarmé duly proposed a toast, now as presiding honorand rather than 'humble admirer', and did so in the form of a Petrarchan sonnet in octosyllabic metre, beginning with the very pun with which he had begun his toast in December – 'verre / vers':

Rien, cette écume, vierge vers
A ne désigner que la coupe;
Telle loin se noie une troupe
De sirènes mainte à l'envers.
Nous naviguons, ô mes divers
Amis, moi déjà sur la poupe

Vous l'avant fastueux qui coupe
Le flot de foudres et d'hivers;

Une ivresse belle m'engage
Sans craindre même son tangage
De porter debout ce salut

Solitude, récif, étoile
A n'importe ce qui valut
Le blanc souci de notre toile.

The poem is based on an analogy between a ship and the table, covered in white linen, and elaborates on the 'verre/vers' pun with a further play on 'coupe' (a champagne glass and a caesura) to transpose the banquet into a metaphor of the dangerous sea journey of poetry. Thus the intoxicated poet, unsteady on his feet like the sailor on a storm-tossed deck, stands to propose a toast not to any individual or even 'auroral youth' but to their common pursuit:

> Nothing, this spume, virgin verse /glass to designate only the 'coupe'; such, far off, a troupe of sirens drowning, many upside down. We are navigating, o my divers friends, I already on the poop, you the sumptuous prow cutting through the billow of thunderbolts and winters; a fine intoxication engages me, unafraid even of its pitching, to stand and raise this salutation – Solitude, reef, star – to whatever was worth the white concern of our canvas.

Mallarmé subsequently placed this poem at the beginning of his collected *Poésies*, as an epigraph entitled 'Salut', and to be printed in italics that might suggest not only the intoxication of poetry but the inebriation of print itself. 'Salut': goodbye from the poet, hello to the reader, a passing salute, and perhaps salvation.

The banquets continued. In April 1893 it was the turn of Verlaine, who was particularly unsteady on his feet. In June Hugo was posthumously honoured at a dinner presided over by Auguste Vacquerie, Léopoldine Hugo's brother-in-law, when Mallarmé and Mendès read some of Hugo's poetry; and in October Heredia, one of the 'ancestors', took the chair. In December, at a banquet in honour of the sculptor Auguste Rodin, Mallarmé and Zola flanked the honorand at the head of the table.

Mallarmé's desire to 'display' his own brand of language in public – to enact the ceremony of the Book – also informs his ongoing commitment to journalism throughout the 1890s, and he is to be seen commenting with ever-growing acuity and urgency on the contemporary cultural and political scene. The precedent of his 'Notes sur le théâtre' (later *Crayonné au théâtre*) prompted an offer from W. E. Henley, editor of the *National Observer* in London and a friend of Whistler's, to engage him for a series of articles (in French) on the Parisian cultural scene. From March 1892 until July 1893 Mallarmé wrote on a variety of topics that included the advent of *vers libre*; concerts of ancient music at the Église Saint-Gervais; the book trade; Huysmans' novel *Là-bas* (in connection with a current controversy about black magic); Parisian response to the deaths of Tennyson, Banville, and Maupassant; the Panama Canal scandal that brought disgrace on Ferdinand de Lesseps, erstwhile builder of the Suez Canal; and a number of theatrical events: Loïe Fuller's shows at the Folies-Bergère, the performance of Wagner's *Die Walküre* on 10 May 1893, and the premières of the third part of Dujardin's verse trilogy, *La Légende d'Antonia*, and of *Pelléas et Mélisande*, the Symbolist drama by the Belgian playwright Maurice Maeterlinck that was later turned into an opera by Debussy in 1902.

As these articles suggest, Mallarmé the journalist was still largely the arts critic, but the piece on Lesseps is indicative of a growing readiness to comment directly on contemporary social issues and in particular to participate in an increasingly noisy debate about the relationship between social unrest and recent literary trends. Were Anarchism and Symbolism synonymous? Did the rule-breaking spirit of *vers libre* also inform the actions of men like Auguste Vaillant, the unemployed labourer who had thrown a home-made nail bomb from the visitor's gallery in the Chambre des Députés on 9 December 1893?

An opportunity now presented itself to address this explosive issue within the tranquil curtilages of Oxford and Cambridge. Earlier in the year Mallarmé had received an invitation from the University of Oxford to deliver a lecture on the topic of 'Letters'. He had asked to defer the invitation since he was now in the process of retiring from teaching on the grounds of ill health, and a capacity for foreign travel might rather undermine his case. And he was particularly anxious not to undermine it, having been genuinely troubled for so many years by illnesses that were always real even if they were sometimes convenient. In 1891 he had suffered yet another severe bout of rheumatism and been granted three months' sick leave, followed by a return to school in the autumn on reduced hours and reduced pay. In January 1893 a further month's leave –

Mallarmé's dedication of *Vers et prose* (1893) to Whistler, who had provided the frontispiece: 'Whistler – through whom I defy / The centuries, in lithography. – M.'

on the grounds of severe bronchitis – had been granted, fortuitously allowing him time to prepare his poem for the *La Plume* banquet in his honour. But in July 1893 he applied to be relieved permanently of his duties, appending a note from his doctor that itemized neurasthenia, heart problems, dyspepsia (too many banquets perhaps), and persistent insomnia. (The note records also that he measured 1.63 metres and weighed 150 pounds.) He was granted permission to retire on a full pension as from 1 January 1894, after 30 years' service. To this pension, of 2,500 francs, was added an annual state grant of 1,200 francs in recognition of his literary endeavours, subsequently raised to 1,800 in October 1895. So the state did give poets a living after all.

On Thursday, 1 March 1894 at the Taylor Institution in Oxford Mallarmé gave his lecture, entitled 'La Musique et les Lettres', and on the following day he performed it once more at Pembroke College, Cambridge. In a letter home to his wife and daughter he described it as 'a stiff dose of aesthetics' (*Corr.*, VI. 232). Despite genuinely poor health in February he had worked very hard on this text: it was to be a statement of his own poetics and a response to recent attacks on the poets' collective. In Oxford he fell foul of regulations that demanded the lecture be given in English (as well as, if wished, in the original language). His host was Frederick York Powell, an expert in Icelandic and a Student (Fellow) of Christ Church, where Mallarmé stayed . York Powell stayed up half the night to translate Mallarmé's lecture before giving it himself on 28 February at the canonical hour of 5 p.m. Mallarmé gave his own French version at the stomach-rumbling time of 1 p.m. the next day. The composition and lukewarm response of the audiences were disappointing, though one or two native English speakers commented that Mallarmé was less difficult to understand in the French than in York Powell's English. In Cambridge Mallarmé gave the lecture at sunset, between candelabra, to a small and discerning audience (who had paid), and was altogether happier: 'as though Poe had lectured in the presence of Whistler' (*oc*, II. 63).

The lecture, in complex prose, is a mixture of playful wit and serious statement. 'On a touché au vers', the poet mock-portentously begins (after some preliminary remarks about the linked literary traditions of England and France): verse has been interfered with, by *verslibristes* obviously, but also (implicitly) by those who have turned it into a political football. Having asserted his own belief that prosodic order is a *sine qua non* of poetry, even if that order may assume non-traditional forms, Mallarmé broadens his focus by examining the very subject he has been given and poses the fundamental question: 'Does something like Letters exist?' Explicitly rejecting the notion of 'belles-lettres', literature as a form of 'fine writing' that can be aspired to by educated professionals (architects, lawyers, doctors), he asserts something at once more obvious and more far-reaching. The writer must 'piously' observe the letters of the alphabet, 'as they have, by the miracle of infinity, fixed themselves in any one language, his own' (*oc*, II. 66). Guided by a 'feel for their symmetries' the act of writing – 'le vers' – is 'a transfiguration [of letters] into the supernatural term': that is, the creation of a verbal structure or structures ('the turn of such and such a phrase, the loop of a distich': *oc*, II. 67) which are at once 'supernatural', in the sense of being 'above nature', and yet 'copied from our own conformation', and which 'assist the burgeoning, in us, of insights, and of correspondences'. Taken thus, 'Letters' means 'Literature' – and 'correspondence'! – and its purpose is not to describe the world as it is but to suggest 'something else', to 'seize relationships': 'With veracity, what are Letters but this mental pursuit, conducted as discourse, in order to define or to prove, with regard to oneself [us as human beings], that the spectacle [before one] corresponds to an imaginative understanding, it is true, in the hope of seeing oneself reflected in it' (*oc*, II. 68): for example, in the 'symphonic equation proper to the seasons, [the] habit of ray and cloud' (*oc*, II. 66).

This account of 'Letters' is particularly reminiscent of the opening paragraphs of the Villiers lecture, and here is complemented by a comparison with 'Music' that recalls Mallarmé's *National Observer* article on 'Vers et musique'. The lecturer asserts that Music and Letters are two sides of 'of one phenomenon, the only one, I called it the Idea' (*oc*, II. 69). Each borrows from and enriches the other, but ultimately they fuse into one 'entire genre'. The two art forms orchestrate patterns, call it 'Harmony', 'arabesque', or 'silent melodic notation, of those motifs that compose a logic, with our fibres' (*oc*, II. 68). But whereas music 'does not willingly confide', 'Letters' can evoke the whole world, 'the musicality of everything' (*oc*, II. 65). Thus 'I reply with an exaggeration, certainly, and forewarning you of the fact: Yes, that Literature exists and, if you will, only Literature, to the exclusion of all else' (*oc*, II. 66).

Having administered his 'stiff dose of aesthetics', Mallarmé endeavours to lighten the mood by ridiculing the charge that poets like him are either limp degenerates – as Max Nordau had recently claimed in his book *Entartung* (Degeneration) which had just appeared in French translation – or red-blooded bomb-throwing anarchists like Vaillant. Neither analogy, of course, is valid, and taken together they contradict each other. Rather the writer belongs to a minority who regard it as their duty to use everyday language – 'words, the apt words of school, home and marketplace' (*oc*, II. 73) – to communicate a truth that is grounded in universal human experience. For contemporary political leaders are themselves at fault. Whether it be the divine right of kings, the dictatorship of the proletariat, or even democracy, these 'mirages' of the most appropriate form of human association here on earth brutally block from view the possibility of a humanity united in quasi-religious communion with the mysteries of our life on earth: 'the amplification to a thousand joys of the instinct for heaven [*ciel*] that is in each of us' (*oc*, II. 74).

The literary 'minority' of poets, then, is best placed to construct a 'City' in which human beings may live together in harmony and

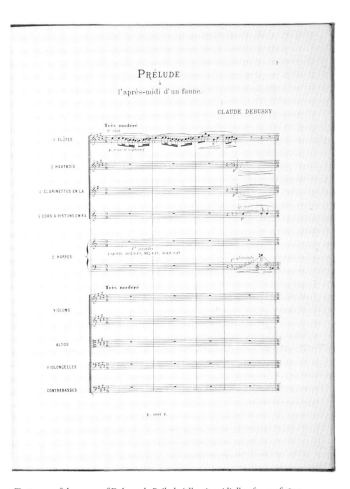

First page of the score of Debussy's *Prélude à l'après-midi d'un faune* of 1895.

a shared spiritual knowledge. As such, society should support them, as Oxford and Cambridge colleges support their Fellows. In an article published in *Le Figaro* on 17 August Mallarmé put forward the suggestion that the law of copyright be altered so that when a work falls out of copyright through lapse of time a royalty should remain payable on the work in question, not now to the owner or heirs of a literary estate but to a 'literary fund', to be administered by the state and offering prizes and grants to young writers. He was serious, but the idea did not catch on. For, to the administrators of the Third Republic, writers both young and old were increasingly suspect, like Félix Fénéon, the faithful *mardiste* who had been arrested and imprisoned for his alleged part in an Anarchist bomb attack on the Restaurant Foyot on 4 April. At Fénéon's mother's request, Mallarmé made an official statement in the young writer's support, which contributed to his acquittal – though he was in fact guilty. But as for Mallarmé himself: 'I know of no other bomb but a book' (*oc*, ii. 660). And on 12 November 1894 he sent his publisher the 'definitive' manuscript of his collected *Poésies*. It would not appear until five years later, posthumously. On 22 December he attended the first performance of Debussy's *Prélude à l'après-midi d'un faune*. The piece was a triumph, but for Mallarmé here was confirmation that poetry could express everything that music expresses and more, much more. The two men were the toast of the town.

7

Dies

Following his retirement from teaching at the beginning of 1894 Mallarmé could be master of his own time, and this had a profound effect on both his public and his private life. From 1895 onwards his visiting card indicated that he was to be found at Valvins 'from May to October' and in Paris during the remainder of the year. At last, like Persephone, he could match his place of residence to the rhythms of the solar year.

The public, Parisian Mallarmé continued to pay homage to fellow poets and artists, whether by banquet toast or celebratory verse. On his return from England in the spring of 1894 he completed his sonnet 'Le Tombeau de Charles Baudelaire': it would appear in *La Plume* on New Year's Day 1895 and again the following year, along with poems by other writers, in the commemorative volume for which it had been intended. On 15 January 1895, once more in *La Plume*, his sonnet in 'homage' to the fresco-painter Pierre Puvis de Chavannes was published in a special issue to mark the artist's seventieth birthday. It was presented to him that evening at a banquet, though Mallarmé did not himself attend.

The Baudelaire poem, provocatively unpunctuated but in traditional alexandrines and Petrarchan sonnet form, honours the urban poet whose *Fleurs du mal* had been condemned by the public prosecutor for their 'poisonous' exhalations. It offers itself instead (in its multiple intertextual allusions to Baudelaire's work) as a conduit for their 'tutelary poison' ('ever to be breathed even

Paul Nadar's photograph of Mallarmé of 1895; he sent a copy of this to Méry Laurent bearing the dedication: 'Monsieur Mallarmé wraps himself in the affection and shawl of Méry' – from whom the shawl was a present.

should we perish from it'), like a street gas-lamp burning its simultaneously deadly and illuminating substance to light up the 'saintly prostitution' of Baudelaire's modern art. The sonnet for Pierre Puvis de Chavannes, also in traditional Petrarchan form and also unpunctuated, employs 'offbeat' heptasyllabic metre to evoke this master of disconcerting allegory and haunting antique scenes. Puvis, the poem intimates, is Moses shepherding the flock of his contemporaries through the wilderness of contemporary mimeticism towards the glorious dawn of a futural beauty that yet has its source in the ancient, founding principles of visual art; a Moses preparing to smite the rock (cf. Pierre [Peter]) from whence will gush the water with which to toast the naked nymph of the ideal. Alluding thus to Puvis de Chavannes' well-known depictions of toga-clad women beside fountains and springs, the sonnet celebrates a timeless pictorial art that is at once classical in its observance of the past and yet radically modern in its flat, two-dimensional technique that rejects all suggestion of mimetic *trompe-l'œil* by eliminating shadow and relief.

In both poems Mallarmé blends poetic convention and innovation to present fellow-artists as themselves 'interregnant', mediating between the 'desuetude' of tradition and the 'preparatory effervescence' of the avant-garde, lighting the way towards a new dawn. As in 'Le Tombeau d'Edgar Poe' the Mallarméan poet presents himself as humble ventriloquist – a medium – defending his honorand against 'blasphemy' and espousing his transgressions. In the Baudelaire poem the shocking phrase 'l'immortel pubis' (the immortal pubis) speaks for all that is scandalous in *Les Fleurs du mal*, while in the homage to Puvis de Chavannes the first tercet becomes a mini-fresco:

> *Par avance ainsi tu vis*
> *Ô solitaire Puvis*
> *De Chavannes*
> > *jamais seul.*

In advance thus you live [also, you saw] / O solitary Puvis / De Chavannes / never alone.

Despite the innovative and far-sighted nature of his painting, which marks him out from the ruck, Puvis is not so far ahead of his time (nor, on his birthday, so much older than his contemporaries) that Mallarmé cannot join him in an act of poetic solidarity, denying that very isolation by at once displaying it visually in this radically disrupted layout and then surrounding it with the comforting embrace of a rhyme. For the great artist, like the solitary word that awaits its rhyming partner, is 'never alone'. Just as he took the torch from another within the lineage of 'prophets', so there will be another to whom to hand it on.

Edgar Degas, *Mallarmé and Renoir*, 1895, photograph.

Mallarmé continued to experiment with layout a fortnight later, on 2 February, when he was invited back by the headmaster of the Collège Rollin to a dinner in his honour. Plainly another sonnet was called for, this time in the 'lower key' of the Shakespearean form. So (as the poem recounts) the retired teacher, playing on his dubious reputation as the author of *L'Après-midi d'un faune*, holds

Edgar Degas, *Geneviève and Marie Mallarmé*, 1895, photograph.

his glass of wine aloft, laughing like Bacchus amidst this potential if unlikely orgy until his host cuts him short with a headmasterly look. The interruptions – as he rises to his feet, as he suffers silent mock rebuke – are figured in the written text in the same way as Puvis' isolation: by the interrruption of the verse and its continuance immediately below on the following line. The extraordinary layout of *Un coup de Dés* was already dawning on the Master himself.

But whereas Baudelaire and Poe were long dead, and Puvis de Chavannes and the schoolteacher's colleagues very much alive, how should Mallarmé respond when a poet or artist underwent the 'solar drama'? Berthe Morisot, at whose house he had dined so often in the company of other painters, died suddenly on 2 March, from complications after catching 'flu from her daughter Julie. Mallarmé sat with her during her final hours. Appointed guardian with Auguste Renoir, Mallarmé became something of a father to Julie, who was still a minor, seeing that she was safely housed with her cousins Paule and Jeannie Gobillard. Their mother,

Yves – Morisot's sister – had died two years earlier. Over the coming year Mallarmé and Julie worked together on preparing a major retrospective of her mother's work, which opened in March 1896: Mallarmé wrote a preface for the catalogue in which he called on this accomplished woman to be recognized also as a Master.

Another close friend, Paul Verlaine, died on 8 January 1896. Mallarmé felt the loss deeply, moved by compassion for Verlaine's vulnerability and disastrous personal life, warmed by affectionate memories of their many conversations and their appalling jokes, and filled with long-held admiration for the man whom he regarded as the greatest poet of their generation. A younger generation had made of Mallarmé and Verlaine respectively the 'leaders' of the Symbolists and the Decadents, but neither man heeded such labels nor such specious division, united as they were by their talented allegiance to poetry itself. At the funeral two days later Mallarmé gave a brief oration, which was published in *Le Temps* newpaper on the following day. Again, as with Poe and Baudelaire, the message is clear: may Verlaine's death put an end to the denigration of this man who has ended up a vagrant drunk befriended by whores, and may his physical absence now permit the voice of his poetry to be heard more clearly, unsullied by irrelevant commentary on the morals of its author.

Mallarmé repeated the message in his verse tribute, a Petrarchan sonnet in alexandrines (with minimal punctuation) entitled simply 'Tombeau', which was published on 1 January 1897 in the *Revue blanche* to mark the first anniversary of Verlaine's death. Here, as in the very short oration that he gave at the graveside on the anniversary itself, Mallarmé sees the acts of mourning and memorial homage as forms of aid: helping the departed to cross 'the shallow slandered stream' of death (*oc*, I. 39) and reassuring his 'shade' as it walks towards the posthumous glory that is the sunshine of the dead. For, as he had expressed it at the beginning of his memorial tribute to Théodore de Banville in 1892: 'the cheerful immortality of a poet resolves the questions, dispels their blur, with a ray' (*oc*, II. 141).

In characteristic fashion, therefore – and as at the time of Villiers' death – Mallarmé responded to loss and grief with practicality, with words of purpose spoken and written that a painter's excellence be acknowledged and truly *seen*, and that another man's words be heard and read unto eternity. Indeed, and perhaps in memory of his friend, he now accepted an invitation from Harrison Rhodes (*mardiste* and publisher of his verse postal addresses two years earlier) to write a piece on Rimbaud for *The Chap Book*, where it appeared on 15 May 1896. In this the most heavily biographical of his prose tributes to other writers, Mallarmé seems intent on conferring existential substance on this 'meteor' (*oc*, II. 121) whose unique genius flared so suddenly and so brilliantly, and exercised 'so particular an influence' on the literature of his time – and on Verlaine.

What Mallarmé could not immediately countenance, by contrast, was another banquet. When *La Plume* organized a dinner on 27 January 1896 to proclaim him 'Prince of Poets', in succession to Verlaine, he declined the invitation. Though he felt out of courtesy that he could not decline the honour, he hated the very title (and the opportunity it offered the press once again to ridicule him for his alleged obscurity), but above all he thought the proposed banquet an unsuitable way to celebrate the life of someone who had known such penury: 'one cannot appropriately, even through the presence of friends, have the death of Verlaine ending in a banquet' (*Corr.*, VIII, 50). Nevertheless when Gustave Kahn celebrated the publication of his latest collection of verse with a dinner, Mallarmé was there once more, on 14 February, ready with a brief prose tribute in which he remembers Kahn as the first of his generation to attend his *mardis*, and (generously) as the first exponent of *vers libre*. A week later his prose tribute in honour of Émile Verhaeren was read out at a dinner in Brussels to launch the Belgian poet's latest work.

In these tributes, ephemeral as they may now seem, Mallarmé was in effect honouring and supporting with this own growing prestige that 'literary minority' to whom he had attributed such a vital social function in his Oxford and Cambridge lecture. In his article on magic for the *National Observer* in January 1893 he had already asserted that human physical and spiritual needs are met in two ways: by political economy and by aesthetics. In the realm of the former, 'credit' has become the new alchemy, the philosopher's stone of capitalism whereby base metal is sometimes 'magicked' into untold wealth: 'With what disorder that is sought, all about us and so little understood!' (*oc*, ii. 251). But this 'dream' is a perversion of human spirituality, a beguiling mirage that we are led to 'credit' when actually we seek some more reliable focus in our anguished human search for value: the sun-gold not of a trillion empty noughts but of art's bountiful 'glorious lie'. 'Everything comes down to Aesthetics and Political Economy' (*oc*, ii. 76), he repeated in the notes he added to *La Musique et les Lettres* on his return from England; and he proceeded to address the issue.

Early in 1894 he had been approached by Thadée Natanson, editor of the recently founded *Revue blanche*, to write a series of articles on the role of the poet in modern society. Entitled *Variations sur un sujet* they appeared from 1 February to 1 November 1895, and they form a logical sequence of parts that Mallarmé later redeployed in *Divagations*. The first *Variation* – entitled 'L'Action' (later 'L'Action restreinte') – sets up the series by simulating a meeting between the poet and a younger, aspirant poet who seeks his advice on what a poet should *do*: to wit, avoid ephemeral engagement and work for the longer term (as discussed above in 'Critical Moments'). In subsequent articles Mallarmé examines in turn, and from the perspective of his own aesthetic: contemporary debate about an 'intellectual aristocracy' both as a replacement for the Church and as an antidote to the vulgarization allegedly consequent on democratic rule; Huysmans' novel *En route* (written in the aftermath of his conversion) and the role of religion in a French society shaped by the secularism initiated by the 1789 Revolution; the role of the French academy as a guardian of the French language; the value of music in combating the alienation of urban populations by reflecting the rhythms of nature in city concerts; a comparison of the book and the newspaper; the class struggle; poetry as a superior form of music; the relative roles of the labourer and the poet as 'workers'; and the 'solitude' of the poet, avoiding the compromising 'prize-giving' culture of bourgeois capitalist society while nevertheless fulfilling a fundamental social role in offering the 'crowd' a means of quasi-religious solace.

In January 1889 Mallarmé had voted for Georges Boulanger, the revanchist right-wing general and Minister for War who just then was at the height of his popularity. But he had done so expressly on behalf of Geneviève (women did not get the vote in France until 1945). Mallarmé himself cared little for party politics, and in so far as he had political sympathies they were clearly republican and to the left of centre. Nevertheless he was as suspicious of socialist and communist ideology as he was of reactionary aristocrats and priests, and the *Variations* are the work of a poet who seeks to transcend social divisions through an appeal to the universal power of language, and of poetry in particular, to address and salve our alienated humanity.

Mallarmé immediately reworked these articles (along with those he had written for the *National Observer* in 1892–3) for inclusion in his collected prose works, published by Edmond Deman on 15 January 1897. As Mallarmé points out in his own blurb, these 'ravings' actually demonstrate 'the extent to which a frank and perspicacious writer acquired a notoriety quite at odds with his true qualities simply because he excluded clichés, found the right shape for each sentence, and practised purism' (*oc*, ii. 1610). The title *Divagations* is also modestly disclaiming, evoking a putative randomness in the collection that Mallarmé deplores in the three italicized paragraphs with which he introduces it: 'A book of the kind I do not like, diffuse and devoid of architecture.' He blames this on the inherently 'journalistic' nature of much of its contents, playing on the double meaning of 'jour' in French (day, daylight) to imply that from within the mess of the day-to-day he may nevertheless have brought certain truths to light. Perhaps, indeed, there is a hidden unity. Leaving aside the prose poems with which *Divagations* begins, he says, the remainder 'treats of a subject, of thought, [that is] unique'; and Mallarmé compares the whole to a cloister which 'though ruined, would exude, for the walker, its doctrine' (*oc*, II. 82).

Divagations opens with Mallarmé's thirteen prose poems, under the heading 'Anecdotes ou poèmes'. Thereafter the wandering visitor to the 'ruined cloister' is led away from the external world of 'anecdotal' narrative and through a series of sections: first, texts that focus on other writers and artists; then the essay on Wagner, which leads on to *Crayonné au théâtre* and its presentation of Mallarmé's own views on theatre and opera, culminating in his eulogy of Banville's verse drama; then 'Crise de vers', where the focus shifts fully onto poetry and its role at this time of crisis; and then four sections – 'Quant au livre' (As for the Book), 'Le Mystère dans les lettres', 'Offices', and 'Grands faits divers' (Major News in Brief ') – in which Mallarmé arranges his *National Observer* and *Revue blanche* articles as a carefully structured exposé of his own 'doctrine'.

The three texts within 'Quant au livre' address the realities of book publishing and the Press, and we learn how the book, as a 'spiritual instrument', can draw inspiration from the typographical procedures of newspaper layout and so match format to content (as *Un coup de Dés* will soon do). In 'Le Mystère dans les lettres', originally a response (in 1896) to Proust's attack on what he claimed were the wilful neologisms and semantic obfuscation of Symbolist poetry, Mallarmé explains his conception of poetic 'mystery'. His own work is 'obscure', he contends, only if one approaches it as though one were reading a newspaper: i.e. for unambiguous information. As a writer he has scrupulously observed the rules of syntax (the 'guarantee' of intelligibility), but his reader must envisage the act of reading as a process of transition. Beginning with the blank contingency of the white page we trace the sequence of verbal elements and pursue a coherence by inferring the silent connections between them ('chance conquered word by word'). At the end we have simply the text ('nothing beyond it') and a whiteness of page that is now filled with the 'authentic' presence of the implicit, of the myriad interconnections silently filling the interstices of the 'poem'. The 'virginity' of the silent page has been sundered into 'fragments of candour' (etymologically, 'whiteness'), 'nuptial proofs of the Idea' (*oc*, II. 234).

In the three texts grouped as 'Offices', the writer is likened to a musical conductor or religious celebrant, the reader to a participant in a ritual act, akin to the Catholic Mass, which potentially unites all readers in a communal, therapeutic enactment of the solar rhythm. Finally, in the nine texts grouped as 'Grands faits divers', the poet presents himself as the most effective guardian of value in this time of crisis. The Panama Canal scandal has exposed the destructiveness of capitalism (ruining thousands of small investors); anarchist bomb attacks maim and demolish; black magic perverts the spiritual. Yes, music – in the form of the popular concert (like Paris's Concerts Lamoureux and London's Proms) – can restore a sense of the pastoral and the 'bucolic' to the alienated urban dweller, but how much more powerful is poetry in its evocation of human experience at its most fundamental, 'rhythmic' level and yet also in the complexity of its semantic articulations.

In 'Confrontation' (the seventh of the 'Grands faits divers'), Mallarmé weighs his own worth against that of a manual labourer, presenting himself as no less of a 'worker' and one, moreover, who is denied the daily satisfaction of a job well done. As he struggles with the 'impossibility' of the poetic task, the poet is his own cruel and unforgiving taskmaster, seemingly condemned forever to start again, eternally unpaid. Moreover – as shown also by the prose poem 'Conflit' (Conflict) – it is his function not simply to 'dream', but to provide symbolic explanations that will serve a social function in illuminating the endless round of manual labour as a version of the solar cycle. And an imagined handshake of mutual recognition signals the end of this 'confrontation', for writing, too, is a form of manual labour.

The 'Grands faits divers' section ends with 'Sauvegarde' (Safeguard), in which Mallarmé attacks the Académie Française, that venerable institution founded in the seventeenth century for the purpose of governing and defending the French language by producing a dictionary. Yet its forty 'Immortal' members are remiss, spending their time in idle ceremony and otiose discussion, whereas the true guardian of the French language is the writer, the 'literary minority'. Mallarmé ends this text, and therefore *Divagations*, by calling on the Academicians to come together as 'one hero', as a guard of honour, and to put their forty 'frail' swords together in the symbolic shape of a bird's wing. But the implication is plain. The poet's pen is mightier than the ceremonial sword, and with it he wields mankind's most potent means of responding to the world around it: the word. On the wing of language the human spirit soars.

Following publication of *Divagations* Mallarmé became once more the focus of ceremonial tribute. On Tuesday, 2 February 1897 the poet Paul Valéry organized a dinner for younger *mardistes*, though it caused so much friction among the faithful (some older *mardistes* had not been invited) that Valéry himself very nearly did not come. The 36 guests who did attend were met by a floral display in the shape of a lyre, bearing the initials SM. On 23 March (another Tuesday, of course, but also five days after his 55th birthday) the 'Prince of Poets' was presented with an album of 23 poems by his friends. The Belgian writer Albert Mockel had distributed to each of them a sheet of finest vellum, bearing a watermark featuring an olive branch and the sacred initials. Their handwritten poems were bound, in alphabetical order by poet's name, in a shiny folder of morocco leather, complete with clasp and decorative naiad.

And so it continued. In 21 April 1897 Mallarmé attended a private concert given by the young Venezuelan-born pianist and song composer Reynaldo Hahn, recently Proust's lover and now the protégé of Méry Laurent (a year later she would make him the executor of her will). Doubtless at her instigation Mallarmé penned an introductory speech, to be read out by the Comédie-Française actress and so-called 'muse of the Symbolists', Marguerite Moréno. In his short, carefully wrought tribute he praised Hahn for his talent in setting poetry to music, a rare accolade from a man who believed that a poem already contained its own silent music, its sacred song – or 'mystery' (*oc*, II. 691). And on the following evening he gave the toast at a dinner in honour of Catulle Mendès . . .

Unsurprisingly, therefore, this public, Parisian Mallarmé was also the man who simultaneously hankered after the quiet waters of Valvins. Thanks to his retirement he could now spend increasingly prolonged periods of time there, sometimes on his own and relying on a maid, Lucie, to cook and clean for him. In November 1895 the owners of the house agreed to let further rooms in the property for an increase in rent of 200 francs per year: two additional rooms on the first floor, adjacent to the two rooms that had hitherto served as the bedroom and sitting-room of the Mallarmés' exiguous holiday home, plus two on the ground floor. Marie and Geneviève would share a bedroom facing east over the garden to the rear, while Stéphane chose a bedroom-cum-study commanding a view of the river and the forest and sunsets beyond. The poet's enthusiasm for interior decoration found new expression as he determined that each room should have a special colour-scheme of its own, each one a 'surprise' (*DSM*, II. 102). The ladies' room would be a pale green, his own a delicate grey. The kitchen was enlarged, and the sitting-room with its stylish red wallpaper was redesigned to give pride of place to their cherished eighteenth-century porcelain clock, a symbol that Valvins was now the Mallarmés' principal residence.

In principle he retreated to Valvins to get on with his writing, but, as his daughter rightly commented, he was no recluse. A growing community of writers and artists had taken up residence along the banks of the Seine. The artist Odilon Redon, whom Mallarmé had known since being introduced to him by Huymans in 1884, lived nearby with his wife and their son Ari, to whom Geneviève had become godmother in 1889. Mallarmé had always felt particularly in tune with Redon's art ever since the latter had sent him a copy of his *Homage to Goya* (in 1885). Of the six lithographs that comprised it, Mallarmé particularly valued the one figuring a man's thin, melancholic face, with a clenched fist pressed pensively to his lips, against a backdrop striped with darkness and light:

> my entire admiration goes directly to the great Magus, bent on the inconsolable and obstinate pursuit of a mystery that he knows does not exist, and which he nevertheless seeks after, only ever that, from within the grief and mourning of his lucid despair, for *it would have been* the Truth! I know no other drawing that conveys so much intellectual fear and awful sympathy as this grandiose countenance. (*Corr.*, II. 280; Mallarmé's emphasis).

In Redon's company Mallarmé made the acquaintance of other local artists, notably Pierre Bonnard and Édouard Vuillard. And then there were his old friends the Dujardins who regularly invited him to dinner at their home just down river at Samois (Dujardin would also bring him regular supplies of his favourite tobacco from Paris). The Irish novelist George Moore recalled meeting Mallarmé there in April 1897 and hearing him sketch out a work in progress:

Mallarmé and
Méry Laurent
in 1896.

'a man loves a woman and is about to marry her; but the seed which
is in this man (the potential child within him), dominated by the
thought that its potential mother will have to lose her virginity, tries
to dissuade his potential father from marrying' (*OC*, I. 1393). Moore
took this as evidence of a Mallarmé who continued to be haunted
by the 'to be or not to be' of *Hamlet*, and a surviving fragment of
manuscript, now known under the title of 'Épouser la notion'
(Espousing the Notion), shows the poet playing once more with
the paradox of virginity (at once perfection and sterility) that had
once informed his *Hérodiade* and soon again would.

On one treasured occasion in May 1897 Méry Laurent came to
visit, accompanied by her maid. Lodging nearby for three nights,

she happily participated in her host's favourite walks, visited his favourite places, lunched and dined alone with him at Valvins. Mallarmé made no attempt to hide the visit from his wife and daughter, who were still in Paris, and each kept her silent counsel on the matter. But when Marie and Geneviève were present, other female guests would visit, like Julie Manet and her Gobillard cousins. Though Mallarmé himself kept his commuting to a minimum, the train service enabled many *mardistes* to visit the Master in his rural retreat: Rodin, for example, or the recently widowed Whistler, who came down in October 1897 and painted a delightful pastel portrait of Geneviève. Paul Valéry was an increasingly frequent visitor, especially if he thought Jeannie Gobillard might be present (they later married). But he complained in July 1897 that he and Mallarmé always drank too much when they were together, and admitted sheepishly that their conversation sometimes tended to the smutty. The elder poet had taken to the younger as to the son he might still have had.

During the more sober moments of their conversation the two men discussed Mallarmé's latest work, the extraordinary poem entitled *Un coup de Dés jamais n'abolira le Hasard*. A version of this had recently appeared in the international review *Cosmopolis* on 4 May (alongside a poem by Rudyard Kipling and some unpublished letters by Turgenev and Nietzsche), a foretaste of the fine-art edition for which his publisher Ambroise Vollard had just given him a 250 francs advance and which was to be published in a print run of 200 at 50 francs per copy. Mallarmé suggested that Odilon Redon should provide the illustrations. Ever since the 1860s Mallarmé had seen poetry as a kind of textual theatre, linguistic acts or events performed before the reader's gaze during which individual words and syllables manifested evolving patterns of sound and meaning until the last syllable brought a closure of sorts: a 'final point that consecrates it', we read at the end of *Un coup de Dés*. Since 1886 he had been experimenting with unpunctuated sonnets in which

Geneviève Mallarmé at Valvins in 1896.

stanza, metre and syntax hold the words in tremulous suspension upon the page. At the same time, and since the early 1870s (and *La Dernière Mode*), he had been developing a prose style in which insistent but highly unconventional punctuation serves a concerted deployment of subordinate phrase and clause that disturbs conventional linearity of exposition and creates a no less tremulous deferral of meaning. Now in *Un coup de Dés* he created a text whose true title (since it comes first, in bold capitals, on the first page) may be 'Poème': a fashioning of language in which words and phrases have been released from the grip of stanza and justified margins and now are situated at various, seemingly random positions on a double-page spread, like stars in the sky. There they hover, in differing font sizes, roman and italic, capitals and lower case, bound together by syntax alone.

The *Cosmopolis* version had necessarily been constrained by the dimensions of the journal page, whereas in the proposed Vollard edition – of which Mallarmé had already shown Valéry the first proofs at the end of March – the poet could present the text as he wished. Playing with the numerical possibilities of two dice, and with the idea that two printer's dies have stamped the twin pages of a double-spread, Mallarmé creates a text consisting of 6 folded sheets of paper, producing twelve double-pages and twenty-four sides. The title-page ('POEME. *Un coup de Dés jamais n'abolira le Hasard* par STÉPHANE MALLARMÉ') is intended as integral to the work itself, which thus bears printed text on all 24 sides except pages 2, 4, and 24. These could, therefore, have accommodated the three illustrations that Redon completed for the work (though four had originally been envisaged). The title-phrase is dispersed in large capitals over pages 3 ('UN COUP DE DÉS'), 5 ('JAMAIS'), 11 ('N'ABOLIRA') and 19 ('LE HASARD'), and is then followed on pages 20–23 by another statement in much smaller capitals: 'RIEN N'AURA EU LIEU QUE LE LIEU EXCEPTÉ PEUT-ÊTRE UNE CONSTELLATION' (nothing will have taken place except perhaps a constellation).

Read as statements about the poetic act itself, these sentences suggest that in the act of writing – as words are cast like dice upon the page – the inherent randomness of language will not be set aside. The linguistic event will have taken place but changed nothing, except that it may have produced a constellation: some random and yet seemingly significant pattern, like the Plough mentioned on page 23 and simulated twice in the disposition of the words at the bottom of that page.

The final 'statement' of the poem, at the very bottom of page 23 – 'Toute Pensée émet un Coup de Dés' (Every Thought emits a Throw of the Dice) takes the reader back to the beginning. Far from being authoritative statements of the Truth, big thoughts – like 'a throw of the dice never will abolish chance' – are in fact merely throws of the linguistic dice. For Mallarmé considered that it was impossible to formulate a thought outside language: 'thinking being to write without accessories' (*oc*, ii. 208). Thus it is possible to read the entire poem as having been 'emitted' by the word 'dé' itself, since in French it means both die (where *dé* derives from Latin *datum*, meaning 'given') and thimble (where *dé* derives from Latin *digitus*, meaning 'finger'). The poet has taken the contingent givens of his own language, its linguistic data, and sown them into 'text', like a sailmaker, in an act of manual labour.

From these and other, connected linguistic data a ghostly narrative emerges from the tumbling, seemingly incoherent words of this poem. A 'Maître' (Master; but also, homophonically, metre) is going down with his ship as it founders in a maelstrom – thus recalling the shipwreck evoked in the sonnet 'A la nue accablante tu . . .' (Kept silent from the overwhelming cloud . . .), recently published in Gustave Kahn's *L'Obole littéraire* in May 1894 and now the butt of Tolstoy's ridicule in *What is Art?* (1897). But this Master is also holding some dice and, on them, 'the unique Number that cannot be another' (i.e. the irrevocable combination that will appear once they are thrown). As he hesitates, Hamlet-like, to throw

SOIT
   que

           l'Abîme

   blanchi
       étale
         furieux
               sous une inclinaison
                  plane désespérément

                           d'aile

                      la sienne
                           par

Double-page spread from the 1914 edition of *Un coup de Dés.*

avance retombée d'un mal à dresser le vol
et couvrant les jaillissements
coupant au ras les bonds

très à l'intérieur résume

l'ombre enfouie dans la profondeur par cette voile alternative

jusqu'adapter
à l'envergure

sa béante profondeur en tant que la coque

d'un bâtiment

penché de l'un ou l'autre bord

LE MAÎTRE

surgi
  inférant

                de cette conflagration

                            que se

                    comme on menace

        l'unique Nombre qui ne peut pas

                                    hésite
                        cadavre par le bras
    plutôt
        que de jouer
          en maniaque chenu
                la partie
            au nom des flots
                                un

                    naufrage cela

Another spread from *Un coup de Dés.*

c   hors d'anciens calculs
          où la manœuvre avec l'âge oubliée

                    jadis il empoignait la barre

à ses pieds
          de l'horizon unanime

prépare
    s'agite et mêle
        au poing qui l'étreindrait   .
un destin et les vents

être un autre

              Esprit
                  pour le jeter
                          dans la tempête
                  en reployer la division et passer fier

écarté du secret qu'il détient

envahit le chef
coule en barbe soumise

direct de l'homme

            sans nef
                n'importe
                        où vaine

them, he knows that in throwing the dice he will forsake his control over them and become a hostage to fortune as he awaits the outcome of their tumbling. The dice-thrower will 'die' – like Igitur in the early prose text of that title – and become heir to the contingency of his own act, born again in the new present of the dice's eventual stasis. How will they land, these dice? How *would* they land if he were to throw them, for it is not clear that he does. Across the centrefold of the poem (pages 12–13) the typeface changes from roman to italic, suggesting as in the earlier 'Salut' the intoxi-cated swirl of storm-tossed language as well as, here, the tumbling of as yet unresolved numerical combination. The stability of roman type returns on page 19, only to pronounce the inevitable result: 'LE HASARD'.

Thus does the poet 'cede the initiative to words', letting 'dé' write the poem as once in the 1860s he had allowed the letter x or the syllable 'or' to carry him across the sea of the page. But the poet may yet be a Master. 'Metre' may have dissolved in the maelstrom of this ambitious performance of the freest of free verse, but measurement survives. The number six appears to 'haunt' the centre of the poem homophonically ('comme si', as if; *'si'*, but yes), but soon the number seven begins to insist, also homophonically and then in the final disposition of the words on the final page of print (figuring the Plough itself, just as in the 'Sonnet en yx' the double quatrains and tercets of the Petrarchan sonnet mirror its pattern): a mirage of meaning, perhaps, but also a glimmering pattern of necessity.

Part of the originality of *Un coup de Dés* lies in the fact that Mallarmé clearly envisaged it as a multi-media event, for this poem is part fine-art print, part musical score: a minimalist 'total work of art' perhaps, to rival Wagner's. Writing to Gide in May 1897 he stressed the former aspect, noting that he has arranged the words on the page to look like a constellation or a ship listing in heavy seas. The whole point, he says, is that 'the rhythm of a

Odilon Redon, *Sirène*, 1897–98, one of three surviving lithographs he intended for *Un coup de Dés*.

phrase or sentence concerning a particular act or even an object make sense only if it imitates them and must thereby, figured on paper (taken back by Letters from the original print), somehow or other render something of them' (*Corr.*, IX. 172). Later, in October, he wrote to a young *mardiste*, Camille Mauclair, in similar terms, commenting in addition that this was how 'literature *proves itself*, [there is] no other reason to write on paper' (*Corr.*, IX. 288;

Mallarmé's emphasis). And indeed the poem does offer a series of delicately suggestive calligrammatic effects: not just a constellation (page 23) and a ship listing to port and starboard (pages 6–7), but also a bird tilting its wings in flight (pages 6–7), the spiralling chaos of a maelstrom that is also a whirlwind (pages 12–13), and the isolation of a bird's feather floating on the breeze (page 14) like the poet's quill poised above the page. As the feather falls onto a rock, so it seems like the feather on a toque of black velvet (or a quill dipped in the rippling waters of an inkwell); an aigrette perhaps, or a sinuous siren beating the rock with her forked tail. While Redon's illustrations were required if the book was to sell as a collector's item and thus to be published at all, Mallarmé plainly aspired to produce a fine-art volume in which he was the one and only artist.

If the example of print-making (as well as newspaper layout and the new art of the poster) was in his mind, so too was the example of music. In his prefatory note in *Cosmopolis* he explains how the disposition of the words on the page constitutes a kind of score, recording the human thought process in its bare provisionality, as the mind reconsiders and takes things back, or pursues a train of thought at length, or simply goes off at a tangent. Moreover he envisages this 'score' as a possible guide to patterns of intonation in any oral performance (although when he himself read it out aloud to Valéry, he did so in a flat monotone). Once again it is a question of the *Idée* and the 'rhythm between relationships': his endeavour, he says, owes something to contemporary experimentation with free verse and the prose poem, but under the 'influence' of 'Music as heard in the concert hall'. Just as he was seeking to 'take back' elements of the fine-art print, so he describes himself as 'taking back' from music 'several means that seemed to me to have once belonged to Letters'. In particular he has in mind the evolving art of the symphony, and also Wagner's use of the leitmotif (since Wagner's orchestral music was often played at these public concerts). And in the publisher's blurb accompanying the text in *Cosmopolis*, a blurb written by Mallarmé himself, the objective is made plainer still:

> In this work of an entirely novel character, the poet has striven to make music with words. A kind of general *leitmotiv* runs through the poem and constitutes its unity: accessory motifs arise and group themselves around it. The different types of font used and the position of the blank spaces take the place of notes and musical intervals. (*oc*, I. 392)

For this was now the shape that his Great Work was taking. He told Gustave Kahn that he was planning to write nine further poems like *Un coup de Dés*. Similarly he revealed to Dujardin and Ghil that he had in mind a work in twenty volumes, of which four would contain a sequence of statements (or leitmotifs) like 'Un coup de Dés jamais n'abolira le Hasard', while the other sixteen would develop out of these in the same way as the smaller print of *Un coup de Dés* appears to spring from and elaborate the two central statements. On the centrefold of *Un coup de Dés*, which is framed by the repeated phrase '*COMME SI*' (as if), the poem may be offering a description of itself in the phrase '*Une insinuation simple / au silence enroulée avec ironie / ou / le mystère*' (a simple insinuation in [the] silence rolled up with irony or [the] mystery). An 'insinuation' is an oblique statement, as sinuous as a siren's tail, but it means also (in English as in French) the inscription of an act on a register, having the authority of the law and conferring authenticity on the writing so inscribed. As such it is often used, for example, of the registration of wills. For Mallarmé the act of poetic writing is an art of intimation and oblique suggestion, but it is also a kind of lawgiving, inscribed with knowing irony (conscious of its 'fictional' nature') on the Torah-like scroll that is the concentric structure of *Un coup de Dés*: a sacred text of mystery.

As he had put it in his Villiers lecture: 'a summoning of the world to equate its haunting to some rich postulates – enciphered, as its law, on the paper pale at [or 'pale paper of '] so much audacity' (*OC*, II. 23). The 'Glorious Lie' of poetry has an authenticity and an authority of its own.

But before Mallarmé could write nine more 'insinuations', he wanted first to complete *Hérodiade*, which had now lain dormant for some 30 years. Although he had been thinking of returning to this project since September 1886, this renewed impetus derived not only from early retirement but from Oscar Wilde, who – much to Whistler's catty displeasure – had attended one of Mallarmé's *mardis* in February 1891. In 1893 Wilde sent Mallarmé a copy of his play *Salomé*, which he had originally written in French (late in 1891) and which had just been published. The play itself had been banned in London (it was illegal to depict biblical characters on stage), and premiered in Paris only in 1896, with Sarah Bernhardt in the title role. At the climax of Wilde's play Salome kisses the severed head of St John, and this may have given Mallarmé just the symbolic act that would make sense of his own dramatic poem.

He never did complete the work. In the surviving manuscripts it is entitled *Les Noces d'Hérodiade. Mystère* (Hérodiade's Wedding. [A] Mystery [Play]) and begins with a brief *dramatis personae* (Hérodiade, the Nurse, the Head of St John) and a preface, explaining how the heroine is named Hérodiade rather than Salome in order to dissociate her both from the biblical story and from her current iconic popularity, in painting and theatre, as the mysterious beauty who danced the dance of the seven veils. Thereafter come a 'Prelude' in three parts, of which the second is the 'Cantique de saint Jean' (Canticle of St John); a new 'Scène intermédiaire'; and a 'Finale' in two parts. Apart from the already published 'Scène' (which was to come before the 'Scène intermédiaire') only the 'Cantique' is complete.

In so far as one can judge from these texts *Les Noces d'Hérodiade* would have been a dramatic poem focusing on the relationship between Hérodiade and the severed head of St John, itself eventually placed on a golden platter and insistently compared to the setting sun with its halo-like aureole. In the 'Prelude' the Nurse establishes the symbolic scene of this unlikely wedding feast where a golden platter lies on the table catching the dying rays of the sun. On hearing the head of St John sing a canticle recounting the moment of his beheading, the Nurse wonders from whence this hitherto unheard song comes but now discerns the use to which the golden platter will be put. After the 'Scène', in which Hérodiade prepares for her 'wedding' and banishes her Nurse as she awaits 'an unknown thing', comes the 'Scène intermédiaire', in which the Nurse hides in order to witness what follows, and then the two-part 'Finale', in which (in the first part) Hérodiade calls on the severed head of St John to speak, perhaps to reveal the 'mystery' of what happens after death. In the ensuing silence Hérodiade wonders if by kissing this head she might gain access to this mystery; and this hypothetical event (as hypothetical as the dice-throw in *Un coup de Dés*) modulates into a form of sunset consummation, with the blood from the severed head suggesting the rupture of a hymen. Through her sudden 'haunting' by this face, the virgin princess is enabled to 'open' and 'triumph as a queen'. In the second, much less developed part of the 'Finale', Hérodiade reflects on her new status as 'a female child . . . attentive to the [now] illuminated mystery of her being'. As in *Un coup de Dés* an event has occurred that is at once a death and a rebirth, here explicitly mirroring the solar drama. For Hérodiade, the emblem of beauty, to move beyond the sterility of a virgin purity, she requires to confront – and be seen by – the face of death. Similarly the poem, for it to be a poem, must leave the poetic mind and submit itself to the page, thereby submitting also to a potentially sullying union with the gaze of the reader.

The 'Cantique de saint Jean' consists of fourteen rhyming couplets arranged unconventionally in seven quatrains of three six-syllable lines (like half-alexandrines) followed by a four-syllable line. The effect of this innovative form is thus one of a repeated cutting short – of the twelve-syllable alexandrine that seems to rhyme prematurely, of the six-syllable line as it shrinks to four syllables. These prosodic features complement a poem that starts with a description of the sun beginning to sink from its midsummer and midday zenith (the Feast of St John falls shortly after Midsummer's Day). In the following stanzas, in the first person, the head of St John narrates the moment of its execution (a severance that ends its 'old discords with the body') and tells how it refuses to follow in the direction of its own upturned gaze (fixed on the icy reaches of eternity) but instead tilts forward, as though being baptized, in bowed salute. In death the head seeks no illusory afterlife but rather – accepting the very principle of baptism and renewal that is the 'principle that chose me' – accepts its role in the solar drama of decline and auroral resurrection. The flesh-and-blood St John who dies has become the Baptist, the Precursor, the one who comes before – and whom Hérodiade awaits, 'attentive to the illuminated mystery of her being'.

Part of the reason for Mallarmé's failure to complete the rest of *Hérodiade* lay in his physical condition. Already in the spring of 1897 he had begun to complain of general tiredness: he can just about summon the energy to paint the garden bench and chairs ready for a new season, but the boat can wait. The summer passed in a gentle sequence of visits received and paid, and some work on the proofs of *Un coup de Dés*. In June he wrote to Edvard Munch to thank him for the portrait the Norwegian artist had left for him at his flat in the rue de Rome. During this time the mystery of *Hérodiade* may have deepened slowly. On 7 November Mallarmé was back in Paris, dining at Méry's. The usual round of social engagements followed, including many concerts and a performance of

'The boat can wait': the view upstream from Mallarmé's house at Valvins, with his sailing-boat moored to its pontoon against the backdrop of Valvins bridge and the forest of Fontainebleau.

Wagner's *Meistersinger* at the Opéra on 4 December. In January 1898 he shares with Méry his admiration for Zola's stand in the Dreyfus Affair and his famous article 'J'Accuse' published in *L'Aurore*. In February he writes to Zola expressing sympathy after his prosecution for libel. At the same time he continues to reply dutifully to the many books he continued to receive, like the collection of poems sent by Stefan George and entitled *Das Jahr der Seele* (The Year of the Soul): 'Here you attribute seasons to your soul; excellently, since all poetry however intimate is played out within the spectacle of some ideal year' (*Corr.*, x. 86).

But the year 1898 proved far from ideal. During the spring and summer he worked on *Hérodiade*, but he felt increasingly weary. He had no desire to go boating, and his insomnia was worse than ever: 'I just can't understand it' (*Corr.* x. 203), he told Geneviève in May, shortly before travelling up to Paris to escort his wife and daughter back to Valvins for the summer months. When Valéry visited on 14 July he found his mentor out of sorts and looking very pale. In August Mallarmé responded to yet another of the many 'surveys' that were then popular in newspapers, which sought to boost sales by seeking the opinions of the famous on all manner of phenomena. Tobacco, anarchy, the bicycle (and what women cyclists should wear), top hats, Zionism, Scandinavian literature, cats, Voltaire, Tolstoy, the spring, what 'superior intellectuals' dream about . . . the list was endless. This time the topic was: 'My Ideal when I was 20'. In his brief response he notes: 'the act, chosen by me, has been to write'. It is for others to say if he has realized his ambition. But he adds: 'I stayed sufficiently true to myself for my humble life to have retained a meaning . . . Happy or vain, my will survives intact' (*oc*, II. 672-3). Poignantly this closing use of the present tense does not quite redeem the finality of the past historic ('je me fus fidèle').

At the beginning of September he complained of a sore throat. His doctor diagnosed tonsillitis. But on Thursday, 8 September he suffered a severe choking fit, which may not have been the first. The next morning the doctor called to see his patient at eleven. As they conversed in the presence of Marie and Geneviève, Mallarmé suffered another glottal spasm, and collapsed in front of them. To their very great astonishment he was dead. The funeral took place two days later. On a very hot day Mallarmé was buried next to his son Anatole in the cemetery at Samoreau, in the presence of his close family, Julie Manet and her cousins, and many friends, old and new (Mendès, Dierx, the Dujardins, Thadée and Misia Natanson, Renoir, Heredia, de Régnier, Marguerite Moreno . . .). A number had come by train from Paris, others from the close neighbourhood. One or two of the younger and more fashionable mourners arrived by bicycle, including Alfred Jarry, whose play *Ubu Roi* had scandalized its Parisian audience during its one performance two years earlier. He was wearing women's socks, borrowed from his friend, the writer Rachilde, herself a keen cyclist. Henri Roujon, one of Mallarmé's oldest and most reliable

The lacquered cabinet in which Mallarmé accumulated 'half a century's worth' of notes and work in progress.

friends, gave a short eulogy on behalf of the older generation. Valéry, for the younger, began to speak also, but his words disintegrated into grief.

That evening Geneviève found an empty envelope lying on her father's desk: 'Recommendations regarding my Papers (For when my darlings shall read them)'. A few days later, having doubtless needed time to summon the courage, she explored further and discovered, tucked into the blotter, the letter that was destined for the envelope. It had been written on the eve of the poet's death:

Mother, Vêve,

The terrible choking fit I have just had may recur in the night and carry me off. So it will not surprise you to learn that I am concerned about that pile of notes of mine, half a century's worth. They will simply be a great nuisance to you, especially as not one page of them will serve any useful purpose. Only

Marie and Geneviève Mallarmé in mourning in 1898.

I would be able to make something of them . . . And I would have done so if I had not been betrayed by this loss of my final few years. Therefore, burn them: I'm afraid, my poor dears, they contain no literary heritage. Don't even ask anyone to look at them; and resist all interference, whether kindly meant or simple curiosity. Say they're just a muddle, which indeed is true. As for you, my poor grieving souls, the only creatures in the world sufficiently capable of respecting a lifetime's sincere commitment to art, believe me when I say that it was all going to be very fine.

So I am leaving no unpublished work other than a few bits and pieces that have already been printed, as you will see, plus the *Coup de Dés* and *Hérodiade*, finished if fate allows.

My verse is for Fasquelle here [in France], and Deman, if he is content to restrict himself to Belgium: *Poésies* and *Vers de circonstances* [*sic*], with *L'Après-midi d'un faune* and *Les Noces d'Hérodiade.* Mystery. (*OC*, I. 821)

Geneviève, who took the lead, found herself in an impossible position and sought advice from Paul Valéry, who came down to Valvins on 6 October to inspect this non-existent 'literary heritage'. Together they opened Mallarmé's treasured Japanese cabinet and took out the contents of its many drawers, tantalizing custodians to the mysterious compartments of his mind. It is not known what – if indeed anything at all – was burnt. A sizeable collection of notes has survived to intrigue posterity, beguiling some into unwisely believing that they are in the presence of the Book itself, the Great Work that Mallarmé had envisaged since his mid-twenties. Some pages point to the arithmetic calculations that may have under-pinned the complex structure of *Un coup de Dés* that Mallarmé had intimated to Valéry. Others sketch a number of scenarios that bear faint echoes of *Hérodiade*, while still others suggest preoccupation with a symbolic drama of cosmic dimensions. But, as in Mallarmé's final letter, 'mystery' must have the last word. It is what he would have wished. For now it was his turn to bow his head in submission and undergo the baptism of posterity.

Epilogue: Beyond the Indies

'As into Himself at last eternity changes him.'

('Le Tombeau d'Edgar Poe')

The last poem that Mallarmé published during his lifetime, in April 1898, was itself about a journey into the future. Written for the Queen of Portugal at the invitation of the writer and political commentator Juliette Adam, the Petrarchan sonnet in octosyllabic metre commemorates the moment, four centuries earlier, when the Portuguese explorer Vasco da Gama first rounded the Cape of Good Hope, thus instituting a passage to the fabled riches of the Indies:

> *Au seul souci de voyager*
> *Outre une Inde splendide et trouble*
> *– Ce salut soit le messager*
> *Du temps, cap que ta poupe double*
>
> *Comme sur quelque vergue bas*
> *Plongeante avec la caravelle*
> *Écumait toujours en ébats*
> *Un oiseau d'annonce nouvelle*
>
> *Qui criait monotonement*
> *Sans que la barre ne varie*

*Un inutile gisement
Nuit, désespoir et pierrerie*

*Par son chant reflété jusqu'au
Sourire du pâle Vasco.*

To the sole concern of voyaging beyond an India at once resplendent and obscure, may this salute be the messenger of time, itself the very cape that the stern of your ship is now rounding: just as though, on a yardarm plunging low with the caravel, frolicking in the foam, a bird of new tidings were to issue monotone cries – without the helm shifting – communicating redundant navigational bearings [also, the superfluous whereabouts of riches]: night, despair, rocks [also, precious stones], reflected by its song even unto the smile of Vasco the pale.

In this ironic, self-deprecating poem, the poet compares his own song to the useless cry of a sea-bird and points out the obvious: that memorials, however innovatively written, are of absolutely no interest to the dead, who do not change course. Yet by its very existence the poem salutes a communality of purpose between the living and the dead: the ongoing human quest despite the blackness and the reefs that threaten. As the departed sail off into the unknown, so we and they wonder what lies 'beyond': beyond death – which for some, is a 'cape of good hope' – and beyond the knowable. What *has* the head of St John the Baptist seen? The poem is at once a tribute to past achievement and a celebration of the unceasing human impulse to go forward and discover, to venture beyond even the mystery of the Indies, perhaps even to attempt the impossible Book. Mallarmé and the ghostly Vasco are like ships that pass in the darkness of time, and the French poet offers a naval salute to his fellow-traveller and to a smile that may bespeak the triumph of discovery and progress.

But this Valvins boatman whom Manet had nicknamed the 'Captain' and this poet whose work is filled with nautical and cartographical imagery now lay at rest on the banks of the Seine at Samoreau while his literary self began to navigate the uncharted seas of posterity. At the helm stood his daughter Geneviève. On 20 June 1901, at the age of 36, she married Dr Edmond Bonniot, who was five years her junior. An expert in the new field of radiology, he had been a loyal *mardiste* since 1893. After Mallarmé's death Valéry had raised money from friends to enable Marie and Geneviève to retain their apartment in the rue de Rome, but now an increasingly ailing Mme Mallarmé moved with the newlyweds to a flat near the Parc Monceau. She died there on 6 January 1910, at the age of 75. In 1904 Edmond and Geneviève Bonniot acquired the property at Valvins. Furniture from the rue de Rome was brought there, including many of the sacred accoutrements of the Tuesday ritual, and Geneviève made of her father's room a discreetly commemorative shrine.

Mallarmé at the helm of his sailing-boat on the Seine.

Over a period of twenty years she and her husband supervised the publication of Mallarmé's work. Deman had published the *Poésies* in 1899, in France as well as Belgium, but the Bonniots now looked to Gaston Gallimard, through whose agency a new edition of the *Poésies* was published by the Nouvelle Revue Française in 1913. Vollard had abandoned plans for fine-art editions of *Un coup de Dés* and *Hérodiade*, but the former now appeared, unillustrated, in 1914, also under the imprint of the Nouvelle Revue Française. Work on the Mallarméan heritage was interrupted by the Great War, during which Bonniot served as a military doctor; and on 25 May 1919 Geneviève Mallarmé died, of cancer, and was buried beside her father, mother and brother at Samoreau. But her husband continued the work they had begun together, overseeing the publication of the *Vers de circonstance* by the Nouvelle Revue Française in 1920. Other works followed, including *Igitur* in 1925.

His dying wife had advised Bonniot to remarry, even suggesting a name, Louise Sacquet, the niece by marriage of Mallarmé's pupil, Willy Ponsot, at whose mother's house in Honfleur the Mallarmés had once enjoyed their summer holidays. He married her on 27 November 1920. But his work as a radiologist (for which he was appointed to the Legion of Honour in 1928) took its toll, and he died at Valvins, of cancer, on 2 November 1930, aged 61. His widow lived on at Valvins until her death in 1970 at the age of 84. Following Edmond Bonniot's wishes the house was inherited by her great nieces, Mme Jacqueline Paysant and Mme Marie-Thérèse Stanislas, from whom it was acquired in 1985 by the Département de Seine-et Marne and successfully converted into the present-day Musée Départemental Stéphane Mallarmé. This opened in 1992, 150 years after Mallarmé's birth. As he would have wished, it is no mere monument to the dead (though it does contain an archive) but a living place to which the public is welcomed, especially schoolchildren, and in which regular exhibitions continue to relay the torch of art.

Commemorative plaques were affixed beside the doorway of 89 rue de Rome in June 1912 and to the house at Valvins in October 1923, but it is Mallarmé's work that most eloquently carries on his name. After Bonniot's death the corpus was taken in hand by his friend and colleague, Henri Mondor (1885–1962), a professor of clinical surgery. Mondor edited it for Gaston Gallimard's Bibliothèque de la Pléiade, in collaboration with the noted translator and lyricist Georges Jean-Aubry, and after the interruption of another war Mallarmé's *Œuvres complètes* finally appeared in 1945. (Mondor succeeded to Valéry's chair in the Académie Française the following year.) This edition served Mallarmé's memory well for over half a century before it was replaced in the Bibliothèque de la Pléiade, on the centenary of his death, by Bertrand Marchal's authoritative two-volume edition (1998–2003). Meanwhile Mondor had begun work on editing Mallarmé's correspondence (which Mallarmé had very expressly not wanted published), at first with the literary critic Jean-Pierre Richard (b. 1922), and then with the Australian-born Cambridge professor Lloyd James Austin (1915–94), who, after Mondor's death in 1962, carried the work through to completion over some three decades.

Mallarmé's physical belongings and his written work have therefore been well cared for. What, though, of his name? The first wave of posthumous critical reception manifested itself largely in memoirs, as *mardiste* after *mardiste* published accounts of their meetings with this man who had come to occupy almost all points on a scale stretching from sanctity to insanity. For some Mallarmé was the man who had envisioned a work of literature so radical and so profound that no mere mortal could write it; for others he was a hoaxer, concealing vacuity beneath a monstrous carapace of nonsense. In the former camp Paul Valéry was a key heir. He himself had been rendered speechless, not just at Mallarmé's grave but for the next 22 years, during which he published no further poetry. It was as though he had been silenced by the extraordinary vistas of poetic possibility that a trusting, paternal Mallarmé had revealed to his mind's eye. Above all he seems to have inherited from his forbear the idea that a poem is never finished, only abandoned: a glimpse of a 'beyond' that is never quite within reach.

The prospect of the Great Work dominated Mallarmé studies for many years, cloaking him in the Romantic persona of the doomed genius engaged in a 'search for the absolute' (as the title of one of Balzac's novels has it). Mallarmé himself, of course, tended to present himself to others in these very terms, as in his stated predilection for the Redon lithograph that figures 'the great Magus, bent on the inconsolable and obstinate pursuit of a mystery that he knows does not exist'. And it does seem from all the accounts left by *mardistes* that he could play this part to perfection. But there was also substance in this prospect. One *mardiste*, Édouard Dujardin, wrote to Mallarmé in January 1887 apologizing for his own outburst the previous Tuesday: 'the extraordinary, the unique magnificence of your thought caused such a strong reaction on my part. For it is nothing short of a religion that you have in mind' (*Corr.*, iii. 84, n. 1). Similarly Valère Gille, writing in *La Jeune Belgique* in March 1890, recorded a conversation with Mallarmé during his Villiers lecture tour:

> he suddenly revealed his conception of Art. With marvellous logic he deduced from it the work that was required, said why he had not wanted to publish *the Book* just yet, and talked to us about the synthesis of man to be condensed into one single poem, a sort of symbol, a spring of truth at which all humanity would come to drink, and how he thought the moment had finally arrived to sum up all the knowledge amassed by our unceasing labour: Art a Religion. (*Corr.* iv. 87–8, n. 2)

But the nature of this 'Book' changed many times over the course of Mallarmé's life. Certainly he seems always to have dreamt of some single work, however multi-volumed, that would indeed 'sum' everything up, and it was with (albeit diminishing) reluctance that he published at all. As he told Edmund Gosse in December 1892:

> I have worked hard, published very little, only what well-disposed publications have taken from me, somewhat by force and very much at random. I would have preferred to maintain a total silence . . . No matter! These fugitive bits and pieces are still very precise reference points on my mind's journey. (*Corr.* v. 176)

In his 'Bibliography' at the end of the 1899 *Poésies* he comments that many of the poems are 'drafts with a view to something better, as one tries out the nibs of one's pen before setting to work' (*oc*, I. 46). This may suggest something paltry and inadequate. But many of the poems are radical, deeply considered and supremely accomplished examples of an entirely new way of writing poetry. As Valéry understood, Mallarmé's relatively small output of poetic work had been enough to cause a fundamental reassessment of the very nature of the 'literary'.

Before and since his death Mallarmé has never ceased to represent a touchstone for other poets, both in France and elsewhere. For Valéry himself the nature of the poetic act had now to be analysed with almost incapacitating precision. Apollinaire and the Surrealists looked to the extraordinary display of *Un coup de Dés* as a deliverance from order and constraint and an intoxicating celebration of chance, while members of the OuLiPo group (Queneau, Perec, Roubaud, among others) have conversely taken their cue from the Mallarmé who used wordplay, prosody and even arithmetic to generate literary pattern with careful calculation. Where Mallarmé had stressed the gap between word and thing, some – like Francis Ponge and Yves Bonnefoy in particular – have sought to forge the strongest of links between poetry and the phenomenal world. Bonnefoy in particular, with his aesthetic of 'presence', continually returns to Mallarmé in

his writings by way of affirming his own poetic project in contra-
distinction to the poet whom he regards as having failed in his
pursuit of the Great Work. From Rilke to Celan in German and,
in English, from Eliot and Pound to Wallace Stevens and Tom
Paulin, Mallarmé's linguistic courage has continued to prompt
poets to 'purify the dialect of the tribe' (*Little Gidding*).

At the same time Mallarmé's example has inflected subsequent
literary theory in important ways. The notions of failure and
impossibility have proved especially and paradoxically rich.
The tantalizing absence of the Mallarméan Book mutated, in
the thought of Maurice Blanchot and the Post-Structuralists, into
an exemplary manifestation of the very impossibility of 'literature'.
Already Mallarmé's own perception of himself as having 'died' and
having 'ceded the initiative to words' had struck a chord during the
early days of Structuralism, when the literary text was seen – by
Roman Jakobson and Roland Barthes among others – to generate
meaning out of a closed verbal system independent of flesh-and-
blood authorial intentions. For Barthes, as for Michel Foucault
also, Mallarmé was ahead of his time in proclaiming the 'death
of the author'. Similarly Mallarmé became an essential reference
point for Jacques Derrida and Julia Kristeva. In *La Dissémination* it
is the Mallarméan text that Derrida chooses in order to demolish
the 'thematic criticism' of the Geneva School (Bachelard, Poulet,
Richard) – with its naive assumption of an unproblematic fit
between word and thing – and to substitute his new concept of
'dissemination' for the suspect 'polysemy'. Texts are not rich clusters
of meaning but – in Derrida's image – dehiscent pods from which
pea-signifieds scatter to the four winds. Mallarmé might himself
have said, as Derrida famously does, that there is nothing outside
the text: just signifiers signifying without origin, without end. For
Kristeva, Mallarmé's orchestration of homophony and rhythm
constitutes a 'revolutionary' insight into the nature of language.
For it brings to the surface a form of 'pre-linguistic' musicality that

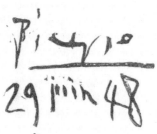

Jean Angladon, *Stéphane Mallarmé*, 1956, woodcut print after Picasso's red chalk drawing dated 29 June 1948.

she associates with the 'semiotic' (evidenced in infant echolalia) and counterbalances the efforts of the 'symbolic' as the ego of syntax and sign does violence to the 'baby-talk' of the id. In Mallarmé, as in the Joyce of *Finnegans Wake*, she bids us hear the voice of a more fundamental signifying.

Beyond literature Mallarmé's presence has been no less felt. Composers since Debussy have wanted to set his poems to music (Ravel, Milhaud, Sauget), and the poet's capacity to raise fundamental questions about the nature and purpose of art – and especially about the role of chance – has been reflected, for example, in the music and writing of Pierre Boulez (especially *Pli selon pli*) and John Cage. In the visual arts *Un coup de Dés* left its mark on the Futurism of Marinetti and the Dadaism of Marcel Duchamp and Man Ray. The so-called 'Concrete Poetry' of the 1950s was its direct heir.

In this sense death is indeed a 'shallow slandered stream', and Mallarmé remains very much alive in the minds and debates of writers, critics and artists across the world. It seems particularly appropriate therefore that in 1948, exactly half a century after the poet's death, Picasso should have considered the absence of a living model no obstacle to his art. Following in the tradition established by Manet, Renoir, Whistler, Gauguin, Munch and others, his simple drawing affords perennial sight of a living Mallarmé, gazing silently into the stillness of mystery and lit by the sunshine of the dead.

Bibliography

Works by Mallarmé

Œuvres complètes, ed. Bertrand Marchal, 2 vols (Paris, 1998–2003)
Documents Stéphane Mallarmé, ed. Carl Paul Barbier et al., 7 vols (Paris, 1968–80)
Correspondance, ed. Henri Mondor and Jean-Pierre Richard (vol. I), Henri Mondor and Lloyd James Austin (vols II–XI), 11 vols (Paris, 1959–85)
Correspondance complète (1862–1871), suivi[e] de Lettres sur la poésie (1872–1898), avec des lettres inédites, ed. Bertrand Marchal (Paris, 1995)
Lettres à Méry Laurent, ed. Bertrand Marchal (Paris, 1996)
Un coup de Dés jamais n'abolira le Hasard, ed. Françoise Morel (Paris, 2007)

Works by Mallarmé in English translation

Collected Poems, trans. Henry Weinfield (Berkeley, CA, 1994)
Collected Poems and Other Verse, trans. E. H. and A. M. Blackmore (Oxford, 2006)
For Anatole's Tomb, trans. Patrick McGuinness (Manchester, 2003)
Divagations, trans. Barbara Johnson (Cambridge, MA, and London, 2007)
Selected Letters of Stéphane Mallarmé, trans. Rosemary Lloyd (Chicago and London, 1988)

Works on Mallarmé

Austin, Lloyd James, *Essais sur Mallarmé*, ed. Malcolm Bowie (Manchester, 1995)

Bernard, Suzanne, *Mallarmé et la musique* (Paris, 1959)

Bersani, Leo, *The Death of Mallarmé* (Cambridge, 1982)

Bonniot-Mallarmé, Geneviève, 'Mallarmé par sa fille', *Nouvelle revue française*, XIV (1926), pp. 517–23

Bowie, Malcolm, *Mallarmé and the Art of Being Difficult* (Cambridge, 1978)

Breatnach, *Boulez and Mallarmé: A Study in Poetic Influence* (Aldershot, 1996)

Catani, Damian, *The Poet in Society: Art, Consumerism, and Politics in Mallarmé* (New York, 2003)

Cohn, Robert Greer, *Towards the Poems of Mallarmé* (Berkeley, CA, 1965)

— ed., *Mallarmé in the Twentieth Century* (Cranbury, NJ, 1998)

Davies, Gardner, *Mallarmé et le drame solaire* (Paris, 1959)

Dayan, Peter, *Mallarmé's 'Divine Transposition': Real and Apparent Sources of Value* (Oxford, 1986)

Derrida, Jacques, *La Dissémination* (Paris, 1972)

Fowlie, Wallace, *Mallarmé* (Chicago, IL, and London, 1953)

Gill, Austin, *The Early Mallarmé*, 2 vols (Oxford, 1979, 1986)

Johnson, Barbara, *Défigurations du langage poétique: La Seconde Révolution baudelairienne* (Paris, 1979)

Kristeva, Julia, *La Révolution du langage poétique: L'Avant-Garde* à *la fin du XIXe siècle: Lautréamont et Mallarmé* (Paris, 1974)

Lees, Heath, *Mallarmé and Wagner: Music and Poetic Language* (Aldershot, 2007)

Lloyd, Rosemary, *Mallarmé: Poésies* (London, 1984)

—, *Mallarmé: The Poet and his Circle* (Ithaca, NY, and London, 1999)

Marchal, Bertrand, *Lecture de Mallarmé* (Paris, 1985)

—, *La Religion de Mallarmé* (Paris, 1988)

—, *Salomé: Entre vers et prose: Baudelaire, Mallarmé, Flaubert, Huysmans* (Paris, 2005)

McCombie, Elizabeth, *Mallarmé and Debussy: Unheard Music, Unseen Text* (Oxford, 2003)

Millan, Gordon, *Mallarmé: A Throw of the Dice: The Life of Stéphane Mallarmé* (London, 1994)

Mondor, Henri, *Vie de Mallarmé* (Paris, 1941)

Murat, Michel, *Le Coup de dés de Mallarmé: un recommencement de la poésie* (Paris, 2005)

Nectoux, Jean-Michel, *Mallarmé: Un clair regard dans les ténèbres: peinture, musique, poésie* (Paris, 1998)

Paxton, Norman, *The Development of Mallarmé's Prose Style* (Geneva, 1968)

Pearson, Roger, *Unfolding Mallarmé: The Development of a Poetic Art* (Oxford, 1996)

—, *Mallarmé and Circumstance: The Translation of Silence* (Oxford, 2004)

Rancière, Jacques, *Mallarmé: La Politique de la sirène* (Paris, 1996)

Richard, Jean-Pierre, *L'Univers imaginaire de Mallarmé* (Paris, 1961)

Robb, Graham, *Unlocking Mallarmé* (New Haven, CT, and London, 1996)

Sartre, Jean-Paul, *Mallarmé: La Lucidité et sa face d'ombre* (Paris, 1986)

Scherer, Jacques, *Grammaire de Mallarmé* (Paris, 1977)

Shaw, Mary Lewis, *Performance in the Texts of Mallarmé: The Passage from Art to Ritual* (University Park, PA, 1993)

Stanislas, Marie-Thérèse, *Geneviève Mallarmé-Bonniot* (Saint-Genouph, 2006)

Steinmetz, Jean-Luc, *Mallarmé: L'Absolu au jour le jour* (Paris, 1998)

Sugano, Marian Zwerling, *The Poetics of the Occasion: Mallarmé and the Poetry of Circumstance* (Stanford, CA, 1992)

Temple, Michael, ed., *Meetings with Mallarmé in Contemporary French Culture* (Exeter, 1998)

Thibaudet, Albert, *La Poésie de Stéphane Mallarmé* (Paris, 1926)

Acknowledgements

I owe a considerable debt of gratitude to the Musée Départemental
Stéphane Mallarmé at Vulaines-sur-Seine for their generosity in supplying
the great majority of the illustrations reproduced in this book, and
in particular to Mme Aubane Lunel for her expertise and unfailing
helpfulness during the choice, digitization and transmission of these
images. I am grateful to Mme Jacqueline Paysant for her kindness in
allowing me to reproduce the eloquent photograph of her ancestor-by-
marriage sailing his boat, as I am also to her sister, Mme Marie-Thérèse
Stanislas, for the gift of her book on Geneviève Mallarmé, which has been
an important source of information and a real source of pleasure. Finally
I am indebted to Vivian Constantinopoulos at Reaktion, for her wise
advice about the kind of biographical study I might aim for, and for her
skill and tact in preventing it from being twice as long.

This book is dedicated to the memory of the late Malcolm Bowie (1943–
2007), Maréchal Foch Professor of French at the University of Oxford, and
subsequently Master of Christ's College, Cambridge. His study of Mallarmé
– *Mallarmé and the Art of Being Difficult* (1978) – is, like all his published
work, a model of subtle intelligence and eloquent expression. The man
himself helped many, many people to round the Cape of Good Hope
and to sail new seas in the direction of the dawn. This book is my salute.

Photo Acknowledgements

The author and publishers wish to express their thanks to the following sources of illustrative material and/or permission to reproduce it.

Bibliothèque Littéraire Jacques Doucet, Paris: pp. 47, 79, 100, 101, 160, 178; Glasgow University Library: p. 169; photo Abel Houdry: p. 205; courtesy of the Musée Mallarmé, Vulaines-sur-Seine: pp. 6, 16, 17, 32, 36, 40, 45, 55, 104, 111, 115, 121, 122, 135, 148, 161, 173, 176, 179, 191, 194–5, 196–7, 199, 205, 207, 208, 212, 218; Musée d'Orsay, Paris: p. 103; private collections: pp. 6, 212; photo Louis Sauvager: p. 115.